ESSENTIAL SOAP MAKING

By Mary Humphrey

and

Alyssa Middleton

Beauty For Ashes Press

Essential Soap Making

By Mary Humphrey and Alyssa Middleton

Coming Soon!

Advanced Soap Making: Removing the Mystery

and

Essential Lotion Making

Editing by Karen Bowlding

Cover Design by Jennifer Smith

Copyright © 2013 by Alyssa Middleton

ISBN-13: 978-0615761008

Printed in the United States of America

Published by

Beauty For Ashes Press

Dedication

To Donna Maria Coles Johnson, without your dedication we would never have met. Thank you for your tireless work to inspire and encourage INDIE's (independent business owners) to reach for their dreams!

Acknowledgements

Mary's acknowledgements:

To my faithful husband, Bob, for supporting me. When you see the sparkle of a dream in my eyes, you have always seen that I have the opportunity to pursue it. Your honesty, openness to share the challenges, and your easy-going nature to not point out when the ideas turn sour, are treasured. Thank you, my best friend.

To my sister, Georgia, for your loving patience and listening ear. Your eagerness to hear about my writing, my business, and farm life, is so appreciated. The saying "sisters are special" cannot even begin to touch who we are, what we share.

To my friends, Bob and John, and others, who realize that I am a person driven to enjoy my dreams. And, a person driven to make a difference in the lives of others. Even though you apply pressure, "You are not allowed to have a bad day," I know those are words of love. Your support never waivers.

To my Heavenly Father, with which I have had a lot of conversations through prayer, I wouldn't be here on my two feet without you. I love you for providing strength when I didn't seem to hold it myself.

Alyssa's acknowledgements:

To my Lord and Savior, words cannot express my thanks for all that You've done: your blessings, your protection and transforming my life. May all I do glorify Your name.

To my parents, Larry and Sandy for steadfastly believing in me and my dreams, no matter how crazy they may seem.

To Tony, thank you for blessing me with our two beautiful children, for being a phenomenal husband and father, and for all the behind the scenes work you do to make my dreams a reality. I am yours forever.

To my children, Alaina and Alijah, thank you for radiating Heaven's joy and light into our daily lives. It is all for you. Mommy loves you to the moon and back.

About the Authors

Your trusted guides in this journey to creating luscious soaps are Mary Humphrey and Alyssa Middleton. Both are experienced at handcrafting body care products and running successful small businesses. We have shared our experiences, tips and tricks to save you time and energy in your soaping journey.

Mary Humphrey

Mary Humphrey is the owner of Annie's Goat Hill. She has been handcrafting soap and personal care products for ten years, and has owned and operated Annie's Goat Hill Handcrafted Soaps for five years. Personal words from Mary, "As I work from Annie's Red Barn studio, I realize the blessings I have in my life. I make the handcrafted soap that I have loved for nearly 50 years. I work with the fragrances that I have always treasured. I also raise animals, which I have always had a deep heart for - goats that I tend to lovingly that supply the milk for my products. As time passed, I gained the desire to share my business and personal knowledge with you, with others. One of my goals in life is to encourage others to realize their dreams. If I can do that today, for you, as you read this book, I have accomplished much of what I have set out to do."

To connect with Mary on social media, please visit:

Facebook: http://www.facebook.com/anniesgoathillhandcraftedsoaps
http://www.facebook.com/maryhumphreyauthor

Twitter: http://www.twitter.com/anniesgoathill
http://www.twitter.com/penandinkspot

Linked In: http://www.linkedin.com/in/maryhumphrey/

Blogs: http://anniesgoathill.com/
http://penandinkspot.com

Alyssa Middleton

Alyssa Middleton is a multi-passionate entrepreneur and author. Not only has she been handcrafting bath and body products for 15 years and has owned Vintage Body Spa since 2007, but in 2011 she opened the Bath and Body Academy to help current and aspiring beauty business owners build their businesses to rapid profitability. She has since expanded her reach even more by starting High Wire in Heels, a website for moms to launch and grow their businesses while raising a family. When soap making, Alyssa prefers making cold process soap and loves creating new essential oil blends to naturally scent her products. Alyssa lives in Louisville, Kentucky with her husband and two children.

To connect with Alyssa on social media, please visit:

Facebook: http://facebook.com/alyssaamiddleton
http://facebook.com/highwireinheels

Twitter: http://twitter.com/highwireinheels

LinkedIn: http://linkedin.com/in/alyssamiddleton

Website: http://www.alyssamiddleton.com

Disclaimer and Terms of Use Agreement

The authors and publishers of this book have used their best efforts in the preparation of this book. The accompanying materials provided are the best practices available at the time of publication. The authors do not accept any responsibility or liability for any damages, loss, or injury arising from use, misuse, or misconception of the information provided in this book. The information contained herein is strictly for educational purposes. If you wish to apply ideas contained in this book, you are taking full responsibility for your actions. While we believe the projects to be safe and fun, all such projects are done at the reader's sole risk.

The authors do not warrant the performance, effectiveness or applicability of any sites listed or linked to in this book. All links are only for information purposes and are not warranted for content, accuracy or any other implied or explicit purpose. The authors have affiliate agreements with some of the websites linked to in this book, and may receive compensation for purchases made through the affiliate link. All rights reserved. No part of this book may be copied or changed in any format, sold or used in any way, under any circumstances without expressed permission from both Mary Humphrey and Alyssa Middleton.

Contents

Introduction 3
History of Soap Making 4
Ingredients Used in Soap Making 8
Liquids 8
Oils 8
Other Ingredients 12
Antioxidants 15
Scenting 15
Other Ingredients Used in Soap Making 18
Basic Soap Making Instructions 19
Before You Start 20
Safety First - Using Sodium Hydroxide (Lye) 21
Steps to Making Soap 24
Using Herb-Infused Oil 40
Coloring Using Herbal Infusions 42
Coloring Using Micas, Ultramarines and Oxides 44
Adding Exfoliants 48
Adding Milk 48
Superfatting 50
Troubleshooting 50
Starting a Soap Business 60
Now What? 60
Things to Do / Needed Items to Open Your Own Business 60
Pricing Your Soap 69
Where to Sell Your Handmade Soaps 74
Resource Directory 78
Glossary 82

Introduction

Welcome, thank you and congratulations on purchasing this book. You're now on your way to learning how to make soap from scratch! We'll teach you several methods of making soap (focusing specifically on cold process soap), ingredients used, techniques and safety as well as a few formulas you can use as a starting point to make gentle, natural soap. Easy to follow step-by-step instructions and photographs are provided.

> Many people, like me are interested in returning to the basics, a simpler way of life. Along with a desire to bring an easier mode into their lives, they strive to use natural soap and personal care products. We hope this book helps you in the endeavors that you have – whether it be to make the soap for yourself, or to sell to a fast-growing community of consumers interested in both handmade and as natural as possible products. – Mary

We've also included a resource directory so that you can quickly and easily find the supplies needed to make and package your products. There are many bath and body supply companies out there, but we have included a listing of only the best that we have found in our years of regularly purchasing ingredients and supplies. Finally, if you would like to start your own business, you'll learn to package, price and sell your soap.

We hope you'll enjoy making cold process soap as much as we do.

Thank you for your purchase, and enjoy!

History of Soap Making

As a generation, we are most definitely in love with soap, especially when it is handmade. Mention soap making to a stranger and watch their level of interest amplify. Perhaps the increased focus is due to an undeniable urge to return to creating things in our own spaces; similar to how our ancestors did many generations did before us.

> I (Mary) personally became interested in soap making through my love of handmade personal care products and natural fragrance, combined with a vision and wonderment of how our predecessors developed soap from crude, but simple, by-products to the much-loved artistic and soothing bars of handmade soap that we know today.

The history of soap making begins with folklore; with the earliest tale of Romans discovering soap around 1000 B.C., in an area called Mount Sapo. The story is not glamorous. It is said that soap naturally developed after rainwater leached through ash from hilltop altars. The caustic liquids that filtered from the ash continued to flow downhill, combining with discarded plant and animal materials, causing a chemical reaction; which we now call saponification (the combination of plant or animal fats with an alkali solution, which forms soap). According to the ancient stories, rainwater caused the soap to seep into rivers and streams where clothes were washed. People noticed that their clothes were much cleaner when washed in water that contained the run-off (soap), hence, the discovery of primitive soap.

Beyond folklore, the earliest documentation of the use of soap is dated around 2500 B.C. The soap was made by combining ash from fires (lye) and goat tallow. At that time soap was used to clean animal hides. The early stone tablet writings do not tell of soap being used for personal hygiene. Historical documents also describe ancient tapestries and fabric being cleaned using mashed vegetable matter from a plant called soapwort (or soaproot). Soapwort is considered a gentle cleaning agent, and is still used in some museums to clean delicate fabrics and surfaces.

It wasn't until later, as depicted in 13th century French history, that soap began to take shape as we know it today. At that time the French began making soap from olive oil rather than animal fat. The French are also noted as the founders of perfumed soaps through the floral infusion of fats, called effleurage. Enfleurage is the procedure of pressing flowers and herbs into fats that have been spread onto boards or planks. The process is repeated several times to obtain the natural fragrances that are extracted from the fats. The procedure is still followed, but not so much for soap making. Around the 13th Century a much milder soap, called Castile, was produced. It was named for the Castile region in Spain where it originated. To this day, Castile soap is popular for its gentle and pure qualities. Castile soap is made from vegetable fats, such as olive oil.

In early American colonies, soap was made at the homestead. Rendered animal fats were boiled and added to an alkaline solution, much like our modern soap making process of adding fats to sodium hydroxide (lye). The alkaline solution was created by leaching rainwater through hardwood ash. Groups of women gathered to make the large batches of soap, usually producing enough soap to last an entire year for many families.

France claims the key to unlocking the door that opened the world to the cold processed method of soap making as we know it today. In 1791, the chemist LeBlanc invented a method that produced lye from soda ash, which gave birth to the ability to produce a nice, hard bar of soap. In 1823, Nicholas Lablanc, a French chemist, determined the chemical nature of fats and outlined the chemistry of soap making. Creating soap by following an exact formula allowed for the large-scale production of soap as an industry.

Soap Making 101

What is soap? The combination of an acid (oils) and a base (alkaline, specifically lye) forms a neutral salt, commonly known as soap. The chemical process that causes the oils and alkaline to make soap is called saponification (oils + alkaline = soap).

Soap is a surfactant that works in two steps. It first helps water to disperse on the skin, instead of pooling into droplets, and then propels dirt and oil away from the skin.

Detergents are also considered surfactants. The value of handmade soap is that it is gentle, unlike detergents. Handmade soap naturally contains beneficial ingredients, such as glycerin, that help the skin retain moisture.

The Four Main Methods in handcrafted soap making are:

Cold Processed – Oils are heated and then cooled to a certain temperature. A lye/liquid mixture is added to the oils to create a reaction called saponification. Soap is formed within 24 hours, and is cured (becomes mild and hardened) within 4-6 weeks. This is the method we focus on in this book, and the method we recommend for beginners.

Hot Processed – Oils are mixed with a lye/liquid mixture and are *cooked* using a slow heat method. This method is often used to reduce the soap's cure time. We do not advise inexperienced soap makers to use this method. Hot process soap making can produce a bar of soap that is less smooth in texture, and is difficult to incorporate certain ingredients, such as milk.

Melt-and-Pour - A premade glycerin soap base is melted and poured into molds. The soap maker can add a range of ingredients, including colorants, fragrance and some additional oils to the melted soap base. Water and milk cannot be added to the premade soap base.

Milled (often called French-Milled) - Pre-made hot process or cold process soap is grated, mixed with liquids, gently heated and pressed into molds. Additional ingredients can also be added to the soap, such as fragrance and some oils. Because the additional ingredients do not go through a heat process, benefits to this type of soap are scent that does not fade, and oils or butters that hold their moisturizing properties.

> I (Alyssa) made my first batch of melt and pour soap in middle school. It was fun and easy to make, but I only caught the soaping bug years later when I first made cold process soap. I had avoided making cold process soap, thinking it was going to be too hard and that I couldn't work with such a dangerous substance like lye. I wish I'd had this book as a resource when I got started! Since then, I've made more soap than I can count, and love the process of mixing ingredients to create something entirely new and unique. Watching the colors and scents change as the soap is mixed and cures never fails to amaze me.

Ingredients Used in Soap Making

Liquids

Water is the most common liquid used in soap making. Milk, beer, wine or juice can be used, but these are primarily for advanced soap making techniques, and go beyond the scope of this book. We briefly touch on a simple format to use milk in soap, but incorporating other liquids will be discussed in more detail in our upcoming book; *Advanced Soap Making: Removing the Mystery.*

We recommend using distilled water, which is inexpensive and easily found at the grocery store. Distilled water is better to use than regular tap water, because the impurities have been removed.

Oils

Any number or combination of oils can be used when making soaps, and each oil reacts differently with lye to create unique properties in soap. Below is a chart explaining different properties and benefits of specific oils and butters typically used in soap making. Learning what each ingredient is good for will help in creating unique formulas based on your specific needs.

There are two types of oils: soft and hard. Soft oils like olive or sunflower are those that are liquid at room temperature. Soft oils contribute to the conditioning factor of the finished soap. Hard oils such as coconut or palm are those that are solid at room temperature. Hard oils help to make a bar of soap hard after it has cured, and most will find that soap made with hard oils tend to last longer than soap with only soft oils. The exception to this is Castile soap, which is soap made from only olive oil. Although Castile soap takes a long time to fully cure (12 weeks or more), the end result is a nice, hard bar of soap.

Most soap formulas use a combination of soft and hard oils, often with a ratio of 60 percent hard oils to 40 percent soft oils. Select your own combination of oils to create a bar of soap with the hardness, conditioning, lathering and cleaning properties you prefer. Superfatting and how it can benefit your soap will be discussed later in the book.

Oil/Butter (Latin Name)	Soap Properties & Tips	Benefits
Almond, Sweet (*Prunus amygdalus dulcis*)	Stable, creamy lather, conditioning bar with mild cleansing. Good as superfatting oil.	Non-greasy oil that spreads easily and absorbs well. Good for sensitive, itchy or irritated skin. Softens and conditions. DO NOT USE IF YOU HAVE NUT ALLERGIES.
Apricot Kernel (*Prunus Armeniaca*)	Stable lather, conditioning bar. Good as superfatting oil.	Light, silky oil that absorbs quickly. Good for all skin types, especially sensitive, dry, and/or maturing skin. Has a short shelf life, and must be refrigerated after opening.
Avocado (*Persea Gratissima*)	Stable, creamy lather. Conditioning bar with mild cleansing. Good as superfatting oil.	Large amounts of vitamins A, D & E, protein and amino acids make this heavy oil great for dry, sun damaged skin, eczema and psoriasis. Penetrates easily and helps regenerate and soften skin.
Canola (*Brassica campestris*)	Stable, creamy lather, moisturizing bar. Use for no more than 50% of formula.	Economical oil often used as a substitute for some of the olive oil in formulas. Provides Omega 3 and Omega 6 fatty acids for healthy skin. Softens and smoothes skin.
Castor (*Ricinus communis*)	Stable, bubbly lather, conditioning bar with mild cleansing. More than 10% will make a soft bar.	Very thick, sticky oil that contains a unique and beneficial mixture of triglycerides or fatty acids. Castor creates a soothing, protective barrier on the skin.
Cocoa Butter (*Theobroma cacao*)	Hard, stable lather, conditioning bar. Great as a superfatting oil.	Solid at room temperature, but melts upon skin contact. Excellent skin softener; not easily absorbed, so it lays down a protective layer that holds in moisture. Known to soothe, soften, moisturize and nourish skin.
Coconut (*Cocos nucifera*)	Hard, white bar, fluffy lather. Using more than 30% can be drying.	Solid at room temperature, but melts upon skin contact. Its strong antiviral and antibacterial qualities are good for healing wounds and dry, itchy skin. Does not clog pores and absorbs easily, leaving a protective layer. Indefinite shelf life.
Grapeseed (*Vitis vinifera*)	Good as a superfatting oil.	Very light oil. Good for acne and oily skin. Absorbs well without feeling greasy. Mildly astringent to tighten and tone the skin. Short shelf life.
Hazelnut (*Corylus avellana*)	Stable, lather, conditioning bar. Use up to 20% of formula.	Light, strong smelling oil best for oily/combination skin. Easily absorbed and slightly astringent. Keeps best in fridge and has a short shelf life. Mix with other oils to detract from the strong smell. DO NOT USE IF YOU HAVE NUT ALLERGIES.
Jojoba (*Simmondsia chinesis*)	Stable, lather, conditioning bar with mild cleansing. Use up to 10% of base oils, or as a superfatting oil.	Not an oil, but a liquid wax similar to our own sebum (skin's natural oil secretion). Great for acne or oily skin, as sebum dissolves in jojoba. Rich in Vitamin E, it absorbs quickly and helps skin retain moisture. Indefinite shelf life.
Lard	Hard white bar, stable lather, conditioning bar. Use at 30-70%.	Inexpensive, semisolid fat that comes from pigs. Used as an economical base for soap making and moisturizes skin.

Oil/Butter (Latin Name)	Soap Properties & Tips	Benefits
Olive (*Olea eurpoaea*)	Stable, conditioning lather with mild cleansing. Formulas with high olive oil percentage take longer to cure.	Moisturizing and mild good for dry, sensitive or baby skin. Has humectant properties, so it attracts and holds moisture and penetrates deep into the skin. Helps soothe itching or inflamed skin. Lower grade (pomace or refined A) versions are recommended for soap making.
Palm (*Elaeis guineensis*)	Hard white bar, stable lather, cleans well. Use around 20-30%.	Also called vegetable tallow as it has similar properties to tallow. Long shelf life and creates a hard bar of soap. Does not provide specific skin conditioning benefits.
Palm Kernel (*Elaeis guineensis*)	Hard, white bar, fluffy lather. Use up to 30%. Using too much creates a drying bar.	Works well in almost any type of water. Offers mild moisturizing properties.
Rice Bran (*Oryza sativa*)	Stable, creamy, conditioning lather with mild cleansing.	A mild oil that is high in fatty acids; perfect for dry/flaky skin. Natural antioxidant, moisturizing and good for mature, delicate or sensitive skin.
Shea Butter (*Butyrospermum parkii*)	Mildly cleansing, stable lather, conditioning bar. Use up to 25% of base oils, or as a superfatting agent.	Solid butter that melts upon skin contact. Excellent for dry, damaged and aging skin. Extremely moisturizing and soothing, and often used to prevent stretch marks. CONSULT WITH YOUR DOCTOR BEFORE USE IF YOU HAVE NUT ALLERGIES.
Soybean (*Soya hispida*)	Hard, white bar, stable lather, conditioning bar. Use up to 50% of formula.	Light, inexpensive oil that easily absorbs and leaves skin smooth. DO NOT USE IF YOU HAVE SOY ALLERGIES.
Sunflower (*Helianthus annuus*)	Stable lather, conditioning bar. Using more than 25% creates a soft bar of soap.	Inexpensive, easily absorbed oil, good for all skin types. Leaves a slightly oily feeling. Helps skin hold in moisture and manufacture new cells. Use high oleic oil, as it is naturally more stable and resistant to rancidity.
Tallow	Hard white, conditioning bar with stable lather. Use up to 40%; more than this creates a brittle bar.	Tallow is the fat rendered from suet (hard, fatty tissue around the kidneys) of cows, sheep, deer, etc. Long shelf life and very economical. Hard oil to use in soaping.
Wheat Germ (*Triticum vulgare*)	Stable lather, conditioning bar. Use up to 15%.	Thick, slightly sticky oil with a distinct smell. Has very high antioxidant properties, and is often added to other oils to extend the shelf life. Great for aging skin, sun damage, scars and stretch marks. DO NOT USE IF YOU HAVE WHEAT OR GLUTEN ALLERGIES.

Other Ingredients

<u>Butters</u> – Many different kinds of butters can be used in soap to add conditioning properties or to produce a harder bar of soap (see table above). Research the different types of butters and the benefits they provide, and if desired, substitute similar butters in your formulas. Use caution if you have allergies; some butters such as shea come from tree nuts and could cause an allergic reaction.

<u>Herbs/Botanicals</u> - herbs or flowers like lavender buds, peppermint leaves or rosemary can be used in soap to provide additional scent, color or scrubbing power. Buy an inexpensive coffee bean grinder and use it only for grinding herbs. This way, your herbs won't smell like coffee and your coffee won't taste like lavender!

Herbs can play a big part in creating unique soaps. Herbs have been used for centuries to soothe or treat various skin conditions, and are easily incorporated into product formulas by a simple herbal infusion technique, which you'll learn about later in this book. Infusions can transfer some of the healing properties of the herb to your soap. You can also use herbs to add bits of color and provide exfoliating benefits to your soap.

Below is a chart of commonly used herbs in soap, their properties and benefits. Learning what each herb is useful for will help in creating unique formulas based on your specific needs. The formulas in this book only use **dried herbs**, not fresh. Water content in fresh herbs might foster the growth of mold and bacteria, so it is best to use fully dried herbs in your formulas.

Herb	Benefits
Calendula (*Calendula officinalis*)	Has anti-inflammatory, antimicrobial, astringent, antifungal and antiviral properties; effective for healing wounds and skin irritations. Useful for disinfecting and treating minor wounds, scrapes, rashes, cuts, insect bites and other skin irritations. Helps to promote rapid healing and prevent scarring.
Chamomile, German (*Chamomilla recutita*) or Chamomile, Roman (*Anthemis nobilis*)	Great in treating minor cuts and scrapes. Have antibacterial and antiseptic properties. Fragrant herb often used for its sedating and sleep-inducing properties.
Chickweed (*Stellaria media*)	Rich in minerals, this herb is excellent for poultices and skin irritations. Relieves pain and stimulates healing immediately upon application. Especially soothing to the skin. Often used for psoriasis, eczema and other skin disorders.
Comfrey root and leaf (*Symphytum officinale*)	Comfrey contains allantoin, which speeds up the natural replacement and healing of cells. Beneficial for inflamed, sensitive, bruised or dry skin. Used to relieve the symptoms of eczema.
Goldenseal (*Hydrastis Canadensis*)	Strong antiseptic and antibacterial properties make this herb useful in treating cuts, scrapes or other minor skin irritations.
Lavender (*Lavandula Angustifolia* or *Lavandula officinalis*)	One of the most recognized herbs, lavender is renowned to soothe nervous tension and promote restful sleep. Its strong antibacterial and anti-inflammatory properties make this ideal for treating skin abrasions and rashes. Promotes healing, prevents scarring and stimulates growth of new skin cells.
Marshmallow Root (*Althaea officinalis*)	Relieves irritation by coating inflamed surfaces. Used to soothe inflammation, rashes, burns, insect bites and stings.
Plantain (*Plantago major*)	Known in folklore as "Green Bandage," as it is one of the best poultice herbs available. Great first-aid treatment for infections and skin irritations. Helps speed the healing process. Incredibly soothing to rashes, eczema and sunburn.
Rose (*Rose damascena* or *Rosa centifolia*)	Fragrant petals have sedative, antiseptic and anti-inflammatory properties. Use to induce relaxation and sweet dreams.
St. John's Wort (*Hypericum perforatum*)	Anti-inflammatory, and can help speed the healing of wounds, bruises, scrapes, diaper rash and mild burns.
Slippery Elm (*Ulmus fulva*)	Long used to treat itchy, inflamed or irritated skin along with cuts, scrapes, scratches and minor burns. High in minerals. It helps soothe inflammation rashes, eczema and fungal infections.
Yarrow (*Achillea millefolium*)	A strong natural astringent, often used in natural first-aid kits to disinfect cuts and wounds. Sometimes used for mild cases of eczema.

Waxes – waxes are used to produce a harder bar of soap. Beeswax is the most common type of wax found in soap formulas. If you're making vegan soap, one with no animal products or byproducts, candelilla wax or carnauba wax can be used in your formula. Candelilla and Carnauba are twice as hard as beeswax, so you'll need to use less of these waxes in your formula to ensure your bar of soap isn't too brittle. You will need to experiment with your formula if using vegan waxes.

Exfoliants – these ingredients provide extra scrubbing power and are used to remove dead skin cells. Start with a small amount and increase the amount in the formula as needed. Some options include:
- Pumice
- Poppy Seeds
- Cornmeal
- Ground Apricot Kernels / Walnut Shells
- Jojoba Beads –Note: these are natural jojoba wax esters that are smooth and round; they are often used to avoid any microscopic cuts to the skin that could occur by using pumice or pieces of shells.

Humectants – these ingredients help pull moisture from the air and lock it into the skin. Only a small amount of these ingredients should be used — using too much will make soap too soft and sticky. Two commonly used humectants are vegetable glycerin and honey.

Antioxidants

As you can see from the chart of oils on previous pages, some oils have short shelf lives and can go rancid (spoil) quickly. Adding antioxidants to your formula can help protect against rancidity. Antioxidants are very different from preservatives, and the two should not be confused. Antioxidants help to protect oil from spoiling, whereas preservatives protect against the growth of bacteria, mold and fungus. Soaps do not require preservatives.

Two commonly used antioxidants are Vitamin E and Rosemary Oleoresin Extract (ROE). Vitamin E (Tocopherol) is thick and easily blends with other oils. ROE is a thick, dark, natural extract that takes a little longer to blend with other oils, but works well. It has an herbal scent that is usually unnoticeable in the final product. Some oils are thought to extend the shelf life of other more fragile oils, so you may want to consider using some of the following oils in your formulas: Jojoba, Meadowfoam and Wheat Germ.

Scenting

Either artificial fragrance oils or pure essential oils can be used to scent soap. Fragrance oils are scents that have been created in a lab from a variety of aroma chemicals and essential oils. Many people are allergic to artificial fragrances. Fragrance manufacturers are expected to follow ingredient guidelines and to use ingredients that are within safety guidelines. However, companies are not required by the Food and Drug Administration (FDA) to release a listing of the exact chemicals that go into their fragrance oils.

Essential oils are taken directly from the plant, fruit or herb, and have no added chemicals. They are pure, natural, and concentrated. Essential oils are used in aromatherapy, which is a centuries-old practice of using natural essences to promote mental and physical well-being. Essential oils are more expensive than fragrance oils, but may be worth the additional cost if you prefer a pure an all-natural soap.

Below is a chart of essential oils commonly used in soap and their benefits.

Essential Oil	Benefits
Bay (*Laurus nobilis*)	Primarily considered a masculine scent. Has reviving, clearing and antiseptic properties.
Bergamot (*Citrus aurantium bergamia*)	Bright, sunny scent often used to aid depression and anxiety. Reviving, soothing scent.
Black Pepper (*Piper nigrum*)	Highly stimulant oil that is warming and has slightly aphrodisiac qualities.
Cedarwood (*Cedrus atlantica*)	Familiar masculine scent that is fortifying and calming. Helps instill confidence and reduce fear.
Chamomile, German (*Matricaria chamomilla*)	Soothing, calming and balancing. Calms nerves and soothes anxiety.
Chamomile, Roman (*Anthemis nobilis*)	Calming, soothing and comforting. Deeply relaxing.
Clary Sage (*Salvia sclarea*)	Highly euphoric scent often used to ease depression, anxiety and stress.
Clove (*Eugenia caryophyllata*)	Restoring and stimulating oil that has strong pain-relieving and antiseptic properties.
Coriander (*Coriandrum sativum*)	A gentle oil from the spice family; it is reviving and used to stimulate creativity and boost energy.
Eucalyptus (*Eucalyptus globulus*)	Familiar scent often used as a decongestant to clear and stimulate the mind.
Frankincense (*Boswellia carterii*)	Deeply calming and revitalizing, used as offerings since ancient times.
Geranium (*Pelargonium gravolens*)	Helps balance out moods. Very similar to rose. Have antiseptic, antidepressant and uplifting properties. Creates a sense of security and comfort.
Ginger (*Zingiber officinalis*)	Warming and stimulating; often used to physically and psychologically warm the body and emotions.
Grapefruit (*Citrus paradisi*)	Bright, refreshing scent alleviates stress, tension and depression.
Jasmine (*Jasminum grandiflorum*)	Called "Queen of the Night," as the flower is most fragrant at night. Its floral, exotic notes inspire euphoria and it is used as an aphrodisiac.
Lavender (*Lavandula angustifolia,*	Soothing, calming and balancing to skin and moods. Helps promote restful sleep. Antidepressant and sedative properties.

Essential Oil	Benefits
Lemon (*Citrus limon*)	Bright citrus scent great for revitalizing the mindset.
Lemongrass (*Cymbopogon citratus*)	Refreshing, uplifting and stimulating oil with strong antiseptic and deodorant properties.
Mandarin (*Citrus reticulata*)	Have slightly hypnotic qualities which promote restful sleep. Overall is soothing and cheering.
May Chang (*Litsea cubeba*)	Bright, uplifting scent often used to counteract stress and depression.
Myrrh (*Commiphora myrrha*)	Long history of healing, used in first aid since ancient times. Inspires peace and tranquility.
Neroli (*Citrus aurantium*)	Also called orange blossom. Calming, soothing and uplifting. Beneficial in relieving anxiety and stress.
Orange (*Citrus sinensis*)	Called the "Smiley oil" for its joyful, familiar scent.
Palmarosa (*Cymbopogon martinii*)	Delicate floral scent used in skin care for its skin revitalizing properties. Good in perfume to relieve stress and restlessness.
Patchouli (*Pogostemon patchouli*)	Known as the "hippy" oil. Used extensively in perfume as it adds a sensuous, exotic, erotic note to blends.
Peppermint (*Mentha piperita*)	Refreshing and cleansing, with antiseptic and astringent properties. A bold scent that promotes clarity and alertness.
Petitgrain (*Citrus aurantium*)	Recommended for nervous tension and anxiety. Clears away troubled emotions.
Sandalwood (*Santalum album*)	Gentle, erotic scent that appeals well to both men and women. Strong aphrodisiac properties.
Tea Tree (*Melaleuca alternifolia*)	Powerful microbial activity against bacteria, fungi and viruses. Medicinal and stimulating properties.
Thyme (*Thymus vulgaris*)	Restorative, stimulating scent with strong antiseptic properties.
Vanilla (*Vanilla planifolia*)	Familiar, soothing and comforting.
Vetiver (*Vetiveria zizanoides*)	The "Oil of Tranquility" helps in centering and grounding. Earthy scent popular with both men and women. Deeply relaxing scent.
Ylang Ylang (*Cananga odorata*)	Soothing, euphoric and erotic scent often used to treat anxiety and release inhibitions.

Take the time to research essential oils and learn how each can be used. For instance, lavender essential oil is used to calm and relax and promote deeper sleep. Some essential oils should not be used during pregnancy or with other health conditions. The following are some essential oils that are hazardous and should NEVER be used:

Bitter Almond	Cassia	Mugwort	Pennyroyal
Rue	Sassafras	Wintergreen	Wormwood

Other Ingredients Used in Soap Making

Other ingredients such as stearic acid, sodium lactate and clays can be used in soap. We will discuss these hardening or bubble-boosting agents in our upcoming book, *Advanced Soap Making: Removing the Mystery*.

Equipment/Products Needed

Another great thing about soap making is that it does not require a lot of expensive, difficult to find tools and equipment. Once you have used a piece of equipment for soap making, it should be kept separate from other kitchen utensils and not used for preparing food. The equipment should <u>only</u> be used for soap making.

Because lye reacts with most metals, use glass, enamel, plastic or stainless steel utensils and mixing containers. Do not use disposable materials such as Styrofoam or paper.

Behind safety equipment, a scale is one of the most important pieces of equipment in soap making. Incorrect measurements will lead to a failed batch of soap. Each ingredient reacts with the lye solution at a specific rate, so precise measurement is critical to ensure that saponification occurs. Purchase an electronic digital scale that measure in tenths of ounces.

Additional equipment needed for soap making:
- Measuring cups and spoons
- Lye-resistant container for measuring sodium hydroxide

- Large, lye-resistant container for measuring water and mixing lye solution and for pouring the lye solution into the oils. Lye-resistant containers and materials are: heavy glass (high heat and caustic materials can lead to the shattering of thin glass), stainless steel (aluminum discolors and can causing the leaching of metal that affects the end product), heavy plastics (thin plastics may melt or etch from caustic materials and heat).
- Pot to mix the lye solution and oils, and *cook* the soap mixture. Some use a crock-pot for this purpose.
- Thermometers – the types in the picture here will help you easily determine the temperature of your lye mixture and oils before mixing.
- Spoons - stainless steel, plastic or wooden spoons
- Rubber spatula
- Soap Molds – These can be wooden or acrylic. For the beginning soap maker, one to five pound capacity is suitable
- Blankets or heavy towels for insulating the soap molds
- Cutter/blade to cut the soap loaf into separate bars – these can be straight or wavy, depending on the type of finish you'd like on your soap – smooth or with ridges.
- Cooling racks on which the soap bars will cure until ready to use

Basic Soap Making Instructions

We're sure you're ready to jump feet first into making your first batch of soap, but please take the time to read through all of the instructions and cautions first. Sodium hydroxide is dangerous to work with. Following these guidelines and recommendations will make your workplace a safer environment, and soaping a pleasant experience. Don't let the discussion of lye scare you away from making soap, but rather learn about how to protect yourself while participating in this fun hobby or business venture.

Before You Start

Be sure to use clean and dry equipment and utensils. Be sure to follow Good Manufacturing Practices, which include among other things, sterilization and proper workplace preparation. For more information on Good Manufacturing Practices, visit the FDA's website:

http://www.fda.gov/Cosmetics/GuidanceComplianceRegulatoryInformation/GoodManufacturingPracticeGMPGuidelinesInspectionChecklist/default.htm

The formulas in this book are by weight, not volume. To make sure measurements are accurate, you must tare or zero out the scale *before* preparing to measure out your ingredients. To do this, follow the steps below.

1. Place the empty container that you plan to measure the ingredient in (i.e., a bowl), on the scale.

2. Press "on" or "tare." The scale will set to zero.

3. Put the ingredient into the bowl and the scale will only measure the weight of the ingredient, not the weight of the bowl.

Safety First - Using Sodium Hydroxide (Lye)

Sodium hydroxide (NaOH) is also known as lye or caustic soda. It is necessary for saponification, the chemical process by which oils and lye combine and form bar soap. Without lye, there is no soap. Be sure not to confuse sodium hydroxide with Potassium Hydroxide (KOH), which is used to make liquid soap.

Always purchase sodium hydroxide (NaOH) from reputable resources. Do not use sodium hydroxide products, commonly known as drain cleaners that can be found at hardware stores. These products contain small amounts of dangerous ingredients that are not safe for soap making.

Handle sodium hydroxide and a lye solution (the solution made when lye is mixed with a liquid — water, goat milk, etc.) with care. Sodium hydroxide crystals and lye solutions are very caustic and can easily cause chemical burns.

There are a number of safety tips to remember when dealing with lye:

1. Store lye in a sealed, unbreakable container, and well out of the reach of children and pets. The package should be clearly labeled with the proper warnings: Poison, Harmful if swallowed, Keep out of reach of children, etc.

2. Never handle lye without wearing the proper safety equipment: safety goggles (lye will cause blindness if it gets into the eyes), gloves, mask, long sleeves, pants and closed-toed shoes. To avoid the possibility of a chemical burn if any sodium hydroxide or lye splashes on you, you want to have as much of your skin covered as possible.

3. Only start the soap making process when you have a large chunk of uninterrupted

time. You will need to focus on the task at hand and cannot be interrupted or you will risk making a serious and potentially harmful mistake. As an additional safety measure before you start the process, organize all of your materials and equipment in a manner that will avoid accidents, such as tripping, or spills. Avoid using caustic materials, such as lye, when children are present.

4. Only open the lye container immediately before measuring it for your formula. As soon as you are done measuring, close the container.

5. Work in a well-ventilated area when mixing lye. Lye emits strong vapors. When creating a lye solution, do not stand directly over the mixing container nor inhale the vapors. Wearing a properly fitted facemask with vapor cartridges will protect you from inhaling fumes.

6. Always add lye to your liquid (water, goat milk, etc.). An often-repeated phrase in the soaping world is, "It always snows on water." This helps you remember to pour the white lye flakes into the liquid, rather than the other way around.

7. Lye solution is extremely hot. Use caution when handling the container.

8. Should you come into contact with sodium hydroxide or lye, immediately rinse your skin with vinegar. Vinegar is an acid and it will help balance out the high alkaline level of the lye, which will slow or stop the burning. Then rinse with water.

Disposing of Lye

Lye is considered a hazardous substance and therefore has specific instructions and considerations in how it can be disposed. As hazardous waste, lye is subject to federal, state and local disposal regulations. Be sure to check with your local hazardous waste collection agency to find out the specific disposal instructions for your area.

Do **not** pour lye down your sink drain, into a toilet, on the ground or into the trash. Lye cannot be thrown out with your everyday trash.

When storing unwanted lye prior to disposal, be sure to keep it in a stainless steel container with a tight fitting lid. Do **not** store or dispose of lye in a plastic or aluminum container, since lye can corrode through the plastic or aluminum. Be sure to clearly mark the disposal container with poison warnings and symbols.

Store lye in a secure, locked cabinet out of the reach of children and pets.

Never reuse your lye containers for any other purpose.

> Once I (Alyssa) was in a rush to unmold a loaf of soap and didn't put on my gloves. Being distracted and not watching what I was doing, I didn't see that the soap had lye pockets. I felt my fingertips starting to tingle and then burn uncontrollably as the lye began to eat through the layers of skin. I quickly poured vinegar and water on my hand but the lye had already burned away several layers of skin on my fingers. It took weeks before I was fully recovered and you can bet that I've never gone without gloves again! It is worth it taking the few extra moments to make sure you're protecting yourself.

Steps to Making Soap

Once you get the hang of it, soap making is a fun, fairly straightforward and easy process. It is also a precise process. Inaccurate measurements of ingredients will cause the batch to fail. To prevent injury and a failed batch, undivided attention to your soap making venture is essential. So without further ado, here are the basic steps to making soap. First up is preparing your mold.

Wooden Mold Preparation

1. Line the wooden mold with freezer paper that has a plastic coating. Always line the mold with the plastic coated side up.

2. For the ends of the mold, cut lining pieces to fit and place in each end of the mold. Using your fingers, crease the paper at the bottom of the mold, about ½" from the paper edge. Fold excess paper over the top of the mold.

3. For the sides of the mold, cut pieces to fit and place the lining. Use your fingers to crease the paper at the bottom of the mold. Fold any excess paper over the top of the mold. Smooth out any wrinkles prior to pouring the soap mixture into the mold. Wrinkles in the paper will leave small indentations in the finished soap.

Note: no preparation is needed for silicone molds. Read the manufacturer's guidelines before using the mold.

Soap Making Steps

1. Put on all of your safety gear: goggles, mask and heavy-duty gloves.

2. Weigh your lye into a glass or heavy plastic container. Set container aside.

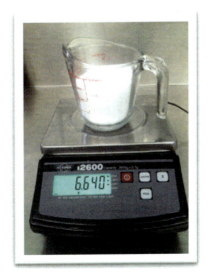

3. Measure distilled water and pour into a glass or heavy plastic pitcher or other container with a pouring spout. It is important to use distilled water because it is purer than tap water, which can contain microscopic pieces of debris and minerals.

4. <u>Slowly</u> pour the measured lye into the water. Stir until all the lye crystals dissolve. The mixture will become cloudy, but keep stirring until the lye is completely dispersed and the mixture becomes clear. Avoid inhaling the emitted fumes during this process. The mixture will also heat up, so avoid touching the mixing container without any protection. Set the lye solution aside to cool while you are mixing the other ingredients.

5. Measure out the remaining ingredients needed for your formula, including fragrances and additives. Measuring everything out in the beginning saves you from overlooking an ingredient, and helps ensure your soap making process will be smooth.

6. Now it is time to melt the oils. First melt the hard oils over low heat. You may be tempted to melt everything on high to speed up the process, but this may scorch the oils. Besides, you need to wait for the lye to significantly cool down, so there is no need to rush this part of the process.

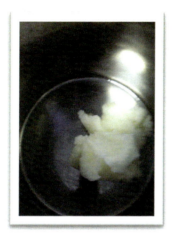

Safety Note: oils can catch fire when they are overheated. The flashpoint (the temperature at which an oil – or any substance - can catch fire) is important to know before heating. Always stay next to your melting pot and monitor the temperature while heating oils.

7. Once your hard oils are melted, add the liquid oils. Stir gently with your spoon.

8. Remove from heat (or if using a crock pot, turn it off and remove the crock from the heating source) and measure the temperature with a thermometer.

9. With another thermometer, measure the temperature of the lye. Ideally, the temperature for both the lye solution and the melted oils will be 100°F. This is a good temperature to start with when making soap. Over time, you may decide to use a different temperature, but for initial batches, stick with 100°F as a rule of thumb.

If either or both the lye solution or the oils are too hot, then place the containers into a sink with ice water. Be sure not to put too much ice water into the sink or it will make the containers float and spill over.

If the oils are too cold, simply return the container to the stovetop or crock-pot and heat until they've reached approximately 100 degrees.

10. Slowly pour your lye solution into the melted oils and stir with a spoon or soap stirrer until you have a uniformly colored mixture.

11. Start mixing with your stick blender.

12. As you feel and see the mixture getting thicker, test the mixture for "trace." Trace is when you turn off the stick blender, lift it out of the mixture and let the soap on the blender head dribble into the mixture below. If the drops sit on top of the mixture for a moment before sinking in, you have reached trace. This may be a fast process or take a while, depending on the oils used in your formula. Stop mixing at this point. You do not want to have thick trace (where the mixture looks like pudding), as this may make it difficult to add in fragrance and/or additives.

Photo timeline of soap mixture coming to trace:

Mixture beginning to thicken

Drizzled soap sits on top for a moment before absorbing into soap mix.

Thick trace, ready to pour

13. Add in any additives. Stir slightly with the stick blender to disperse the additives throughout the mixture.

14. Add in the fragrance or essential oils and stir again with the stick blender until everything is mixed well.

15. Your soap will be thicker now, almost a pudding consistency. It is now ready to be poured. Pour into your prepared mold.

16. When all the soap has been poured into the mold, put the lid on top of the soap (or plastic wrap if a lid is not available).

17. Wrap the mold in towels or small blankets to keep the temperature of the soap from cooling too quickly. If not, soda ash can form. Soda ash is a thin layer of white ash that forms on the top of soap. If this does occur, the soda ash can be cut off, but it is much easier to avoid it in the first place. Keep the soap insulated for about 24 hours. Resist the temptation to peek in on your soap. If you do, trapped heat needed to continue the curing process will be released.

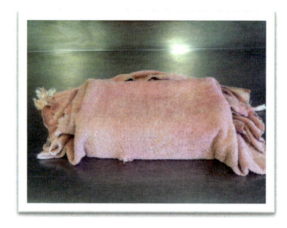

After the soap is poured into the mold, and covered and wrapped, it will go into the gel phase. During the gel phase the temperature of the soap increases and the soap becomes translucent and gel-like in appearance. The gel phase allows the soap to fully saponify, which chemically changes the fats, oils, and caustic materials to soap.

18. After about 24 hours, your soap will be firm in the mold. Carefully remove the soap log from the mold. If you have difficulties in releasing your soap, it may need more time in the mold. Let it sit for another 12-24 hours. If after that time you still cannot get the soap out of the mold, then refer to the mold manufacturer's website to see what they recommend for their particular mold(s); it may be putting the mold into the oven on a low temperature, or some manufacturers will recommend putting their mold(s) into the freezer. Follow manufacturer's directions so you don't damage the mold.

19. Cut your soap into bars using a cutter or blade.

20. Place the cut bars onto a rack to cure. Let the soap cure for 4-6 weeks so that the rest of the water can evaporate and so the soap can become even harder and milder. Every few days flip the bars in a different direction, on each side, to one end, then the other, etc. so that each side of the soap bar is exposed to air during the curing process.

21. Voila! Your soaps are ready!

I (Mary) was extremely nervous the first several batches of soap that I made. I had no idea how long to leave the soap mixture in the molds, what types of soap molds to use, nor did I know how to line them for easy release of the soap. To say the least, it was a blessing to have a curious husband present who was very interested in helping to see that the soap making process became as efficient as possible. We purchased sheets of heavy plexiglass and wood and made soap molds with sections that were supposed to allow the easy popping out of a finished bar of soap. We failed at that attempt when the soap stuck to the plexiglass, and when it broke into several pieces. Then we attempted plexiglass soap towers. We majorly failed at that attempt because we did not insulate the towers, and we left no room for pushing the soap out of either end. Can you imagine using a hammer and a small piece of plexiglass to push the soap out of the mold, for it to only break? It was a funny scene. Thank goodness for a good sense of humor! Finally, we built the wooden soap molds as pictured in this book, and we began using freezer paper to prevent sticking. Remember, your first soap making efforts may result in a gorgeous batch of soap. And if your efforts result in a not-so-perfect soap, then, try again. You'll have a lot of soap on hand for yourself and your family, and you'll learn a lot through trial and error.

Sample Formulas

Simple, One Oil (Castile) Soap Formula

This formula is for Castile Soap, made just with olive oil. Castile soap has been used for hundreds of years and is known for being mild and gentle. When using pomace olive oil in a simple Castile soap formula, the soap hardens quickly and the color can range from a soft white to pale green, depending upon the color of the olive oil.

Pomace Olive Oil	16 ounces
Lye	2.4 ounces
Distilled Water	6 ounces

Note: Various types of olive oil are available to consumers. Pomace olive oil is obtained from the ground olive pulp left over from the first press of olives. While pomace olive oil may not be preferred for cooking, it is a less expensive grade of olive oil and has great saponification values for soap making.

Basic Soap Formula

Pomace Olive Oil	9 ounces
Coconut Oil	4 ounces
Palm Oil	3 ounces
Lye	2.4 ounces
Distilled Water	6 ounces

Basic Soap Formula #2

Pomace Olive Oil	5.6 ounces
Coconut Oil	4.8 ounces
Shea Butter	1.6 ounces
Palm Oil	4 ounces
Lye	2.28 ounces
Distilled Water	6 ounces

Basic Soap Formula - Palm oil free

This formula contains no palm oil. Palm oil is widely used in processed foods, cosmetics, soaps, and other products. The depletion of natural Orangutan habitats, caused in part by palm plantations, has resulted in a rise of formulas that do not contain palm oil, and has led to the awareness of using palm oil that is certified as sustainable.

Pomace Olive Oil	8 ounces
Coconut Oil	4.96 ounces
Shea Butter	3.04 ounces
Lye	2.40 ounces
Distilled Water	5.35 ounces

Conditioning Soap Formula

This formula includes cocoa butter and shea butter for extra moisturizing and a touch of castor oil to boost the bubbles.

Pomace Olive Oil	5.2 ounces
Coconut Oil	4 ounces
Palm Oil	3.6 ounces
Shea Butter	1.6 ounces
Cocoa Butter	0.8 ounces
Castor Oil	0.8 ounces
Lye	2.25 ounces
Water	6.10 ounces

Determining the Volume of a Soap Mold

To calculate the volume of the soap mold measure the inside of the mold as follows:
- Multiply the length by the width by the height (L x W x H) to determine the total volume.
- Multiply the total volume by .40 to calculate the ounces of oils required.

Example:
- The inside measurements of the mold are length 10", width 3", height 2"
- Multiply 10 x 3 x 2 to determine the total volume = 60
- Multiply the total volume 60 x .40 = 24 ounces required in formula (water and lye have been allotted into this formula).

Sizing the Volume of a Soap Formula to a Mold

To recalculate the size of a formula to the size of a mold (using basic soap formula #1) and a mold that requires 24 ounces of oils:

Basic soap formula #1:

Pomace Olive Oil	9 ounces
Coconut Oil	4 ounces
Palm Oil	3 ounces
Total	**16 ounces**

Since the mold requires 24 ounces, divide 24 ounces by 16 ounces = 1.50

Next, multiply each ingredient in the formula by 1.50:

Pomace Olive Oil	9 x 1.5 = 13.5 ounces
Coconut Oil	4 x 1.5 = 6.0 ounces
Palm Oil	3 x 1.5 = 4.5 ounces
Total oils required for mold	**24.0 ounces**

Re-calculate the water and lye according to your new formula. You may use math (in this example 1.5 x the lye or the water) or, for more accurate measurements you can run the oils through a soap calculator, which is discussed below.

Variations

Once you have experience making your first few batches of soap, then it's time to start experimenting! Creating new formulas is one of the best parts of soap making; learning how the different oils combine to create a hard or soft bar, with fluffy or creamy lather.

When testing out new ingredient combinations, be sure to keep detailed notes. If the formula works, you can recreate the soap at a later date. If the new formula flops, then you can review your notes and determine which ingredient might have caused the soap to turn out the way it did.

Any time you are substituting an oil or butter or animal fat into a formula, you will need to run the formula through what is called a lye calculator to determine how much lye is needed to saponify the oil. A couple of online lye calculators we recommend can be found at:

http://www.brambleberry.com/Pages/Lye-Calculator.aspx

Brambleberry also has a Lye Calculator for the iPhone, iTouch and iPad, so if you are interested in having a lye calculator on those devices, visit the iTunes store to purchase that app.

http://soapcalc.net

http://www.thesage.com/calcs/lyecalc2.php

> Allow yourself to have fun testing various formulas. Allow time and freedom for individuality. The formula that you settle on, the one you put the stamp of approval on, will be uniquely yours – one that you love, that your family loves, and perhaps one that your customers come back for time after time. -Mary

Using Herb-Infused Oil

Herb-infused oils are easy to make, and are a great way to incorporate the soothing and healing properties of herbs into handmade products. There are two ways to make herbal oil, and the method you use will depend on personal preference and/or how much time you have.

You will need:

- 1 cup dried herbs
- 2 cups olive oil

Steps for Method #1 – Windowsill Method (infusing rose petals)

1. Place rose petals into glass Mason type jar.

2. Pour oil over petals. Oil should completely cover the herbs, and then some. If more oil is needed, add it to the jar and seal with the lid.

3. Place the jar in a warm area (i.e., a windowsill in direct sunlight) for 48 hours to let the herbs steep in the oil.

4. At the end of the steep, place cheesecloth, muslin or an unbleached coffee filter into a sieve and filter the oil into a clean and dry jar.

5. Squeeze the cheesecloth/muslin/filter well to extract as much oil as possible.

6. Use the infused oil as a portion of or as all of your oil in your soap formula.

Steps for Method #2–Crockpot/Double boiler Method (calendula petals)

1. Place calendula petals into crockpot/double boiler.

2. Pour oil over petals and stir mixture gently.

3. Slowly heat the herbs. Do not let the temperature of the mixture exceed 120°F (50°C). Any higher than 120°F and you will <u>cook</u> the herbs and oil.

4. Let the herbs steep for 2 hours, stirring every 30 minutes or so.

5. Turn off the crock-pot or remove the double boiler and let oil cool slightly.

6. Place cheesecloth, muslin or an unbleached coffee filter into a sieve and filter the oil into a clean and dry jar.

7. Squeeze the cheesecloth/muslin/filter well to extract as much oil as possible.

8. Use the infused oil as a portion of or as all of your oil in your soap formula.

Using herb-infused oils does not change the information entered into a lye calculator. For instance, if you infuse calendula petals into olive oil, you simply select "olive oil" in the lye calculator.

Variations

- Use a combination of herbs in the infusion to incorporate different soothing properties of each herb.

- Make double-strength infusions by taking the infused oils and adding a new set of herbs and repeat the infusion process again. This will strengthen the amount of nutrients in the infused oil.

- Use oils with a stable shelf life: jojoba, high oleic sunflower, coconut, etc.

Coloring Using Herbal Infusions

Herbs can impart a lovely color to your soap, but please note that the FDA has not approved herbs specifically as a coloring agent. Coloring your soaps using herbs is a fairly straightforward process. Simply follow the instructions above to make herbal oil. Start with a light colored oil, such as sunflower or olive oil and infuse the herb of choice into the oil. When the oil is strained, you'll see the oil has taken on the color of the herb/botanical. Use this infused, colored oil as part of your formula. For instance, if your formula calls for 10 ounces of olive oil, replace some of the 10 ounces with the infused olive oil. You will need to experiment with this technique to find the exact amount to use to achieve the shade of color that you're looking for, and take detailed notes so that once you find the perfect shade of color, you'll know how to recreate it.

Note that the color of the soap batter will look different during the mixing process than it will once cured. For instance, using alkanet-infused oil can make your soap mixture look grey in the soaping pot, but when the soap has cured, it becomes a lovely shade of lavender. Refer to the chart below for a listing of some of the herbs or botanicals that can be used to color your soap using this method.

Herb / Ingredient	Color
Activated Charcoal Powder	Black
Alkaneet	Light Pink to Dark Purple
Annatto Seed	Yellow to Orange
Calendula Petals	Yellow to Orange
Chickweed	Green
Cinnamon	Tan to Brown
Cloves	Brown
Comfrey Leaf	Light to Dark Green
Indigo	Dark Blue
Kelp	Green
Madder Root	Light Pink to Deep Red
Nettle Leaf	Bright Green
Paprika	Peachy Orange
Plantain	Green
Peppermint	Green
Pumpkin	Deep Orange
Rosehip Seed Powder	Pink to Tan
Spinach	Green
Spirulina	Blue-Green
Turmeric	Yellow Gold
Woad	Light Blue

Coloring Using Micas, Ultramarines and Oxides

There are many colorants available to the handcrafted soap maker.

Adding colorants results in beautiful hues, swirls (the swirling process will be discussed in our upcoming book, *Advanced Soap Making: Removing the Mystery*). The object of coloring soap, however, is to add enough color to the soap *without creating lather that is also colored,* which can stain your skin or the shower.

Examples of soaps colored with oxides and pigments

To avoid wasted batches of soap, always test small amounts (follow manufacturer or supplier instructions) of colorants and then work your way up in subsequent batches of soap.

Always purchase soap-grade colorants from reputable manufacturers and suppliers. Ensure that the manufacturer or supplier states (in the case of natural colorants - oxides, for example) that all impurities have been filtered from the product.

Pigments

Some natural pigments are available, such as oxides, but most are manufactured in labs that imitate the chemical make-up of a natural product. Pigments are available in both powder and liquid form.

Oxides – A natural colorant obtained from iron oxides. Oxides are stable in cold processed soap. Warning: a little oxide goes a long way in a soap formula. Follow manufacturer's instructions when using oxides in your formula.

Ultramarines – Most ultramarines are stable in cold processed soap. Follow manufacturer's instructions when using ultramarines in your formula.

Other colorant types

FD&C Colorants – FD&C is a classification of lab-created colorants approved for food, drugs, and cosmetics. FD&C colorants are mixed into a water base and can be used in many different soap types, including cold processed soap (check your manufacturer or supplier instructions).

Micas – Are generally not stable in cold-processed soap. Most micas are naturally derived and are pearlescent and light reflecting ground powders. An advanced soapmaker can use a very small amount of mica between layers of cold-processed soap, or even in the soap overall, but this process takes a lot of experimenting and experience. Micas are usually used in cosmetics and melt-and-pour soap bases.

Resulting Color – Some fragrance and essential oils automatically color finished soap. For example, vanilla fragrance can tint a soap tan to dark brown, depending upon the percentage included in a soap formula. Lemongrass essential oil can tint soap a light yellow to deep golden color. Color that results from the chemical process (from fragrance and essential oils) often change during the initial 2-3 days of curing. When you first remove a batch of un-cured soap from the mold, do not be upset if the color isn't what you expected. Give the soap several days, even up to a week, to see what the true end result color will be.

How to add pigments to cold processed soap

1. Follow the manufacturer's instructions. Some pigments disperse in water, others in oil or glycerin.

2. Remove a small amount (approximately 2 cups) of the soap mixture *before it reaches trace* and place it into a measuring cup or suitable small mixing container.

3. Mix the desired amount of pigment (usually ¼ teaspoon or less) with a small amount of water/oil/glycerin (approximately 2 Tablespoons) to ensure any clumps or streaks of colorant are broken up and evenly dispersed.

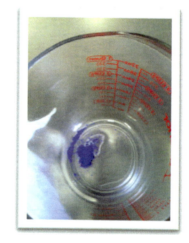 

4. Add the mixed pigments to the small amount of soap in the measuring cup. Use a mixer or stick blender to ensure the colorant is uniformly dispersed.

5. Add the colored soap mixture to the large soap mixture just before the large batch reaches trace, and before fragrance or essential oils are added.

6. Continue standard soap making procedures to finish your batch of soap.

Adding Exfoliants

The easiest time to add exfoliants is when your soap has reached a very thin trace. Add the exfoliant to your mixture and gently fold in until well blended. This will ensure the exfoliant is spread throughout the soap bars. If you wait until the soap is at a thick trace, it may be harder to blend in the exfoliant.

Another way to add exfoliants is to make your soap formula as directed and pour into the mold. Then simply sprinkle the exfoliant onto the top of the soap and gently press (while still wearing gloves and using the back of a spoon). This provides some decoration to your soap as well as making one side of the soap scrubby and leaving the other side smooth.

Adding Milk

Adding milk to soap formulas can create a creamy, luxurious lather. There are many types of milk that can be used, including buttermilk, coconut milk and goat milk, all of which can be found canned, powdered or fresh. Incorporating milk into soap can be a tricky process. Below is a simple method of doing so. Advanced milk soaps will be taught in our upcoming book, *Advanced Soap Making: Removing the Mystery*. In the meantime, if you have questions about using milk in soap, particularly goat milk, Mary is the expert. Please contact her for consulting options.

Simple Method For Adding Milk To Soap

Add milk to the soap formula at a ratio of 25 percent milk to 75 percent distilled water. Example: A non-milk formula includes 6 ounces of distilled water versus a milk formula, which includes 1.5 ounce of milk and 4.5 ounces of distilled water.

Use fresh, canned or powdered milk. If using powdered milk, first reconstitute to a liquid state according to the directions on the package.

Due to the high sugar content in milk, we recommend the 25 percent ratio in a formula to ensure the milk does not scald, or caramelize (turn orange or brown as the soap heats). At 25 percent, the soap will benefit from the milk, but you will encounter fewer problems than by using a higher milk/distilled water ratio.

A pre-preparation step to help prevent scalding of the milk is to freeze the milk/distilled water combination. Break the frozen mixture into chunks prior to adding lye. The lye mixture will then heat and melt the frozen pieces.

Use extra caution when adding an additional ingredient that has high sugar content to a milk-based soap formula such as honey, which can lead to over-heating; dangerously bubbling up, erupting or seizing of the formula.

Note: Refer to the Troubleshooting section of this book for additional help and explanation with potential problems.

Superfatting

Every oil that is a part of a soap formula adds to its beneficial properties; however, even a small portion of oil or butter that is added after the soap reaches trace (after saponification has begun), can add additional moisturizing benefits to the soap. This is called superfatting the soap formula.

Superfatting with expensive oils or butters is often done to help the extra oils hold their original properties.

Superfatting can be accomplished by either reducing the calculated lye requirement by a set amount, or by adding extra oil or butter at trace. A desirable range for superfatting is 3-5 percent; superfatting above 7 percent can decrease the shelf life of a bar of soap, especially when using ingredients that can go rancid.

Troubleshooting

Years of soap making experience don't fully eliminate the occasional finished batch that has imperfections – we've had more failed batches than we'd care to admit! Prevention and a lot of practice is the key to fewer woes in the soap kitchen. This section discusses problems that may occur, how to recognize and avoid them.

Problem: Eruption (Volcano Effect)

Description

Eruption quickly occurs without advanced warning. The soap mixture bubbles up, rapidly grows in size, and erupts into the air or over the sides of the mixing pan. Soap eruptions can happen when the oils are too hot for the lye mixture to be added. The stirring of the soap mixture further increases the temperature. The addition of fragrance oils and additives that contain sugar can also increase the already too hot mixture. Eruption can also occur after overheated soap is poured into the mold.

How To Avoid/Protect Yourself

Check ingredient temperatures *before* mixing (preferably 100°F).

Always cover work surfaces with protective materials such as newspaper or plastic.

Always wear gloves, long sleeves, and safety glasses.

Keep vinegar in the soap making area at all times. Vinegar will help neutralize caustic soap materials and burns on the skin.

Problem: Seizing

Description

Soap mixture thickens very rapidly in the mixing pot, or as it is poured into the soap mold. The mixture thickens to the point it can no longer be poured.

How to Avoid

Check the ingredient temperatures before mixing. Some fragrance and essential oils are sensitive to heat. Always allow the ingredients to cool to the desired temperature before combining and mixing.

Some fragrance or essential oils promote seizing. Always add the fragrance or essential oils at the very end of the mixing process, immediately before the mixture is poured into the soap mold. If you find that a fragrance oil or essential oil causes your soap to seize, then make a note of it. Next time you use the particular fragrance oil or essential oil, try blending it into the soap mixture just before trace is reached to avoid seizing.

When seizing does occur in the soap pot, the soap is not lost. While wearing heavy rubber gloves, spoon the mixture into the mold. Press the seized mixture into the mold with a spoon, spatula or your gloved hands. After pressing the soap into the mold, cover, and allow the soap to set; continuing with standard soaping procedures.

Problem: Mixture will not trace

Description

Soap mixture will not trace during mixing process.

How To Avoid

Some butters and oils will lengthen the time it takes to bring the mixture to trace; an example would be soap that is very high in coconut or olive oil.

The formula may have been measured incorrectly.

If too much liquid and not enough lye is used, the soap may never reach trace, and may need to be discarded.

How do you know when to give up on your attempt to bring soap to trace? When using a stick blender at a steady speed, trace should occur within 15-30 minutes or less. Hand stirring may take hours before trace is reached.

Problem: Mixture separating

Description

Streaking or separating of ingredients during mixing process.

How To Avoid

Some fragrance, essential oils, and pigment or colorants will cause streaking in the soap mixture before they have completely mixed in. Continue stirring.

Dry ingredients, such as ground oatmeal, may sink to the bottom of the mixture if not stirred in properly. Continue mixing to break up and mix the additives. It is best to ensure that dry materials are not clumped or packed before adding to the soap mixture. Only add the materials right before the mixture reaches trace.

Problem: Lumpy Mixture

Description

Soap appears to form lumps while mixing.

How To Avoid

Quick action is necessary.

Lumping most often occurs when the soap mixture is preparing to seize.

Lumping may also occur at trace when a short amount of mixing is still needed.

As soon as you see the formation of lumps, stop stirring with the stick blender.

Immediately, *and slowly*, begin hand stirring to disperse any pockets of fragrance or essential oils or any other additives that may have caused the lumping. If the entire mixture appears to be solidifying, immediately pour or scoop the mixture into the soap mold (see troubleshooting for seizing above).

Signs of Trouble in Finished Soap

For safety reasons, it is *always important to inspect your soap* when you release it from the mold, and again when you cut the soap into individual bars.

Problem: Lye Pockets

Description

Finished soap that contains large or small holes that appears to seep or hold liquids.

How To Avoid

Soap that contains large or small holes that appears to seep or hold liquids must be discarded. The oils and the lye have separated, resulting in lye pockets.

Lye pockets normally occur when the soap mixture is not properly blended before it is poured into the mold. Occasionally an entire batch, or log (or loaf), of soap contains very large tunnels of lye.

Use extreme caution. Wear gloves, long-sleeved clothing and eye protection. Immediately discard the entire batch of soap!

Problem: Hard, Brittle, Crumbly and White

Description

Finished soap that is hard, brittle, crumbly or white

How To Avoid

Hard and brittle soap normally indicates that too much lye was used in the formula. Check your measurements for accuracy. Soap made with too much lye usually isn't mild enough for use on the skin. Discard the soap.

Dry, brittle soap can also result from a formula that contains too high of a percentage of hard oils such as tallow or cocoa butter. Check your formula to see if this might have been the issue.

Problem: Fragrance Too Light

Description

Fragrance too light in finished soap.

How To Avoid

Check the ratios and measurements of the fragrance and/or essential oils that you used in the formula. You may have used too little. Use enough to fragrance the soap, but do not exceed the recommended usage guidelines from the supplier or manufacturer.

Some essential oils, especially those in the citrus family, and some fragrance oils, are not suitable for cold processed alkaline conditions and will evaporate quickly. You can use Litsea Cubeba or Lemongrass essential oils to anchor the scent of Lemon essential oil so that the scent will last longer in the finished soap.

Adding essential or fragrance oils to a soap mixture that is too hot may cause them to evaporate during the soap making process. Always blend at the correct temperature.

Problem: Grainy or "Riced"

Description

Finished soap that appears grainy or "riced."

How To Avoid

Soap that is grainy or appears to be riced is usually an aesthetic issue. The soap can likely still be used, but its appearance may not make it suitable for sale.

Graininess in soap can also be caused by soap that is mixed at too low of a temperature.

Graininess in soap can also be caused by not mixing the formula briskly and consistently before pouring into the mold.

Problem: Soft or Spongy

Description

Finished soap that is very soft or spongy.

How To Avoid

Check your measurements and your formula to ensure it included enough lye.

Continue to allow the soap to cure. The soap may harden over an extended (greater than 4- 6 weeks) period of time. If the soap remains soft or spongy, it can be safely used, however, it may not be suitable for retail sales.

Some ingredients, such as castor oil, some citrus oils and milk can produce a soft soap that takes longer to harden or cure. Allow an additional two weeks of curing time for soaps made with these ingredients.

Problem: Oil on Top

Description

Oil on top of finished soap.

How To Avoid

A very light film of oil, or even droplets, on the top of a newly made batch of soap does not necessarily indicate a problem. If the oil is very thin it will likely absorb into the soap during the cure period.

A heavy film of oil on top of the soap can be caused by any or all of the following: not enough mixing of the batch prior to pouring, ingredient proportions that were incorrect, or a drop in temperature after the soap was poured into the mold.
Check the soap formula and precisely measure the ingredients. Insulate the soap as soon as possible after pouring it into the mold to ensure changes in room temperature do not affect the soap.

Allow the soap to cure for 4-6 weeks. If the soap is mild, meaning there are no holes or seepage of lye affecting other areas of the soap, or hard white spots, soap with a very light oily film on top can be safely used, but may not be aesthetically suitable to sell.

Problem: Cracks

Description

Cracks on the top of finished soap.

How To Avoid

Cracks on the top of soap may be caused by too much lye in the formula.

Cracks can also indicate too much stirring of the soap mixture, causing it to set too quickly.

Formulas with higher proportions of some butters and oils such as castor oil and cocoa butter are more prone to cracking.

Unless the soap also contains white patches (pockets of lye) or if it is too hard or brittle, soap with small cracks is safe for use.

Problem: Brown/Orange Spots

Description

Brown or orange spots appearing in finished soap.

How To Avoid

Brown or orange spots that appear in the soap are an indication of oxidation of excess oils in the soap. This means the oils have gone rancid. Discard the soap.

Excess heat in the curing area can promote oxidation.

Curing areas are optimal at room temperature with average to low humidity. Using a dehumidifier in the curing area with no excess heat helps to prevent brown/orange spots.

Check the soap formula. Ensure that the lye, water and oil proportions are accurate.

Problem: White Film on Top

Description

White film on top of finished soap. This is not dangerous, it can be washed or trimmed off, or used as is.

How To Avoid

Soda ash is a thin white film (only on the top) can be caused by not covering the newly poured batch of soap with plastic wrap, allowing too much air to reach the soap.

A thin white film can also indicate that the soap was made with water that was too hard. Always use distilled water.

A soap formula containing milk often leaves a thin white film on top of the finished soap.

Problem: Turned to Liquid in the Mold or Liquid in Bottom of Mold

Description

Finished soap that has turned to liquid in the mold, or there is liquid in the bottom of the mold.

How To Avoid

The soap mixture reached a false trace and was not properly mixed prior to pouring.

The soap is caustic and **must be discarded**.

Use caution; wear gloves, long sleeves and eye protection while discarding the soap.

Starting a Soap Business

Now What?

So you've been making soap for a while, made some mistakes, had some great successes and you have family and friends telling you to make some extra money by selling your handmade goodness! So how do you do that? This next section will give you an overview of steps to take and things to consider when moving from handcrafting soap for fun to making soap for profit.

Entrepreneurship can be a difficult, frustrating and overwhelming road to travel, but at the same time, there is nothing like making your first sale, receiving large wholesale orders and seeing the gratitude on someone's face... especially when they share that YOUR soap has helped a skin condition they've been suffering with for a long time. Plus, making a living off of your handcrafted work is a pretty amazing feeling as well!

Things to Do / Needed Items to Open Your Own Business

Thinking about all of the steps to take or things you need in order to start a business may seem overwhelming. It isn't bad if you just don't know what to do, and that's why we're here to help! Soap making is a passion of ours and we love seeing others catch the soaping bug and growing to a point where they become entrepreneurs and share their amazing creations with others.

> I (Alyssa) had no business experience and really disliked looking/thinking about the numbers end of a business when I purchased Vintage Body Spa in 2007. It has been an exciting ride, learning as I went along. But if a social worker/mom with no head for business can do this and not only be successful, but also open and run other profitable businesses, you can do this too! Remember the tips and tricks we've included throughout this book have been to help you learn from our mistakes and shorten your learning curve.
>
> Believe in yourself. I believe in you.

Business Planning

First, be sure you have a *lot* of experience making different types of soap. Know that your formulas work and how they work; how they cure, harden and look in 4 weeks, 8 weeks, 6 months or longer. Be realistic. You can't make one batch of soap and suddenly be raking in thousands of dollars in sales each month. But once you create your ideal formula that is fully tested and proven to work, you are well on your way to having a successful business.

Next, think it through. You don't need to write out a formal business plan. That is a misconception that holds many would-be entrepreneurs back from ever getting started. However, take some time to think about and jot down the answers to these five questions:

1. **Why** am I going into business?

Dig deep to really figure out your motivation for wanting to have your own business — beyond "to make more money." Think about and envision what the extra money will do for you and your family: Will it get you out of debt? Will you be able to move to a better neighborhood? Will you leave your day job for a life of flexibility and control of the amount of money you make? Will you be home with your kids instead of paying for daycare?

Being crystal clear on the motivation you have for becoming an entrepreneur will help you stick with it during the tough times. Believe us; they will come. Challenges are inevitable in any business, but holding fast to the vision and dream you have for a different life can give you the strength to carry on, despite any challenges you may face.

2. **What** am I going to sell?

Only unscented goats milk soap? Considering a variety of soaps in different formulas? Will you also offer other bath and body products? What about accessories, such as soap dishes, something that you don't necessarily make, but that can be purchased at wholesale to compliment your soaps. Being clear on what you're going to offer and keeping it fairly concentrated will allow you to develop a clear marketing message.

Also, think about what you're bringing to the marketplace that's unique. Not only will your soap formula be distinctive, but what else will make you stand out in the crowd? **NEVER steal a formula, design, product name, etc. from another company.**

3. **How** will I make money?

Will you create a website and sell online? Will you have booths at craft shows and farmers markets? Will you hold home parties? Sell to boutiques or salons?

You may choose to have multiple sales outlets; this is certainly a way to bring in more money than just selling during farmer's markets, which tend to be a seasonal offering. Take the time to write down the different ways you could make money from selling your soap. Then look at your list and decide which will be the quickest route to profit and start from there. For instance, if it's late September and you have a large inventory of soap that is fully cured and ready to sell, then you wouldn't want to wait until the farmer's market season that starts six months down the road. Instead, you'd want to look at which holiday season craft fairs still have openings and register for booths there. You can start working on a website at the same time. The point is to pick one outlet and just get started. There will always be opportunities and excuses to procrastinate. Just get started!

4. **Who** will I sell my product to?

A common misconception for aspiring entrepreneurs in this field is to think, "Everyone needs to shower and get clean, so I can sell to everyone!" This cannot be further from the truth. Your soap, your packaging, your pricing and marketing message should speak to a specific audience.

Will you serve customers who only want organic ingredients and essential oils? If so, then you won't be making soaps with non-organic oils, artificial colorants or fragrance oils. Do you want to sell to vegans, those who don't use products with any animal products or by-products in them? If so, you'll need to steer clear of animal byproducts, including milk, beeswax, tallow or lard.

You cannot be everything to everyone, so focus on one type of audience for your products and you'll avoid feeling overwhelmed. You can clearly and easily speak to your perfect customers and let them know exactly how your products solve whatever problem or concern they have! When a customer thinks, "Wow, this is perfect for me…I must have it!" it means you've shown that your soap is a great fit for them, and you're on your way to building a loyal customer.

5. **How much** will my product cost?

Again, this goes back to your market, packaging and the message you want to send to potential customers. We'll discuss the different elements that go into pricing your soap a little later in this book and help you determine how to price your soaps to sell *and* make a profit.

While you've been daydreaming about your new soaping venture, you may have started a list of potential business names. Brainstorm as many names as possible, and again, think about the market you will serve, as your company name should be a good fit for that customer base. For instance, if you want to sell only to high end, expensive salons and spas, then you won't name your company "Susie's Affordable Soaps". Not that the name, "Susie's Affordable Soaps" wouldn't be a good fit for another market, but a high end spa will likely respond better to a business name such as "Luxurious Lathers"; a name that speaks to the pampering experience your soaps will provide, or that imply an air of exclusivity.

You may have thought of one or two that sound perfect, which is great! Now, how do you figure out if that name is already taken? Some ways you can search to see if that particular business name is available include:

1. Search for the name using a variety of search engines. See if anyone else has purchased the domain name for that business (i.e., Luxuriouslathers.com). While

Google is the leading search engine, be sure to search other search engines, such as Yahoo, Bing and MSN.

2. Search all social media sites— to see if the name is being used there.

3. Your state's filing office's (often a part of the Secretary of State's office or Department of Revenue) website should have a link to search for registered business names.

4. Your local county clerk's office should have a way to check to see if your desired business name is on a list of fictitious or assumed business names in your county.

5. The United States Patent and Trademark Office (USPTO) at www.uspto.gov has a database of federally registered trademarks that can be searched.

Take the time to search each of the above avenues to ensure the business name you desire is available. Don't just use one search engine and be done with it. You need to be *thorough* and document your searches (i.e., print off copies of your search results) to show that you did not willfully infringe upon another company's trademark by using the same business name. Even with these resources, you may miss a company already using the same name, so it is important to track your search efforts to help show that you did your due diligence in searching for registered or trademarked names prior to filing your business registration paperwork. This may help protect you if another company ever comes to you stating that you're using an already-protected name.

Now that you've found that your desired business name is available, it's time to make your business official.

Discuss with an attorney experienced in small business how to best structure your business (i.e., a sole proprietorship, limited liability corporation or partnership). The primary differences between these structures deal with liability (your financial responsibilities if something where to happen to the business), ownership (who owns the business and who/how many people can invest in the company) and taxation (amount of taxes that will be due and if profits can be *passed through* to the owners before paying corporate taxes first and then be doubly taxed as income tax).

The attorney should also tell you which licenses and permits are required at the state, county and possibly city level, which will be discussed below. S/he may even be able and willing to help complete these registration forms for you.

Licenses, Registrations and Permits

There can be a lot of paperwork to be filed in order to start your business. We don't tell you this to discourage you, but instead to help ensure that you've followed the appropriate steps to starting a business so that you don't run into problems later. Depending on where you live, some of these may not apply to your company. Licenses, permits, and business identification numbers may be required at the following levels:

Federal

A Federal Identification Number (FIN) is also called a Federal Employer Identification Number (FEIN) or a Tax Identification Number (TIN). Don't let the names confuse you. You still need this number even if you do not have employees. As a sole proprietorship, you should get a TIN so that you can use that number rather than giving out your Social Security Number to strangers. You will be often asked for this number. This should be one of the first forms you file. Thankfully, it is a simple and straightforward process that can be handled in one of three ways:

1. Go to the IRS website to complete the online application at https://sa2.www4.irs.gov/modiein/individual/index.jsp.

2. Apply over the phone by calling the IRS Business & Specialty Tax Line at (800) 829-4933 between the hours of 7:00 am and 7:00 pm local time, Monday through Friday. Have the SS-4 form in front of you so that you can provide responses to the questions. A staff member records your responses to the SS-4 form, assigns the EIN and immediately provides the number to you over the phone. If you are in a rush to obtain your identification number, this would be the method to use, as you will not have to wait for an application to be processed and mailed to you.

3. Go to http://www.irs.gov and search for form SS-4, *Application for Employer Identification Number*. Complete this form and submit via fax or mail. The application will be processed and your number mailed back to you.

State

In most states, you will register your business name with the Secretary of State. You may also need to register with the Department of Revenue for a state identification number. Check the websites of these departments for the state in which you live for filing forms and instructions.

You may also apply for a state reseller's license or reseller's permit. If your state collects sales tax, then you may be eligible to qualify for this license. This allows your company to purchase products for sale without paying a sales tax. Since you will not be the end user of the product, your customer is, they would be responsible for paying the sales tax. For instance, if you knew of a woodworker who crafted soap dishes and you wanted to purchase them to sell in your shop, your state may provide you a license so that you do not have to pay sales tax when you purchase those items. Your customer will be charged the sales tax when s/he purchases the soap dish.

County/City

Both the city and county may have separate requirements (and fees!) for business licenses. Call your City Hall and County Clerk's offices and ask what is required to start a business in your city. Even if the company is home based, you will likely need a business license at the city and/or county level.

If you decide to operate your business in another location outside of your home, there will be additional permits and licenses required, including building and zoning permits, among others. Again, your contact at the city and/or county offices will be able to provide a list of what is required.

Insurance

You will need to obtain liability insurance for your company, which will help to protect you should a customer file a lawsuit for whatever reason. Again, we don't mention this to scare you, but rather prepare you for the worst-case scenario; it's best to be prepared and protected. You can search online for liability insurance, but we strongly recommend joining the Indie Beauty Network and/or the Handcrafted Soap Makers Guild, which are discussed in our Resources section. As part of your membership fee to these organizations, you can select various levels of liability insurance coverage.

You may also want to consider obtaining a business rider on your homeowners insurance. This will help to protect your raw ingredients, finished products and packaging and replace these items in the case of theft, flooding, etc., as well as protect your personal finances if a customer were to fall and become injured while coming to your home business to pick up an order. This sort of injury would not be covered by standard homeowners insurance.

Pricing Your Soap

One of the important factors in designing your business structure is pricing. If you calculate your costs and pricing appropriately, and if the price is still reasonable in the marketplace, you'll make a profit. This is where we all want to be…covering our expenses and making money; otherwise, we don't truly have a business, we have a hobby.

Factors to consider in calculating your costs include:

- Raw Ingredients (oils, sodium hydroxide, any additives or colorants that go into your formula)
- Shipping of the ingredients from the manufacturer to your location
- Equipment (stick blenders, molds, curing racks)
- Packaging (soap boxes, shrink wrap, etc.)
- Labels

- Labor: calculate all of the time you spend on making a batch of soap: ordering the supplies, unpacking the order and putting it away, prepping your work area, measuring out your ingredients, making the soap, cleaning up, cutting soap into bars, and packaging and labeling the soap once fully cured. While we may want to pay ourselves $50/hour for our labor, you may find that this greatly increases the final cost of each bar of soap. Be sure to pay yourself a reasonable wage, but not so much that it makes the final price of the soap too expensive.

- Overhead: Overhead is what we call regular expenses that are not directly related to producing your soap, such as rent, utilities, taxes, etc. Other items to consider included in overhead could be:
    - Insurance
    - Website hosting fee
    - Internet fee
    - Phone bill if you have a separate number just for your business
    - Office supplies
    - Banking fees
    - Merchant account / PayPal fees

Instead of pricing out each of these items in your early stages of business, you can simply add a percentage to the cost of goods for each bar of soap to ensure that your pricing covers these expenses as well. Some will recommend starting with a 50 percent overhead to include in your pricing formulas.

- Shipping supplies: when you ship an order to a customer, you'll be responsible for buying the shipping box, the packing cushion or insulation (there are many types on the market) that go inside the box, the label, tape, packing slip and shipping label, as well as postage.

Calculating your costs

We recommend using a spreadsheet program, such as Microsoft Excel to track your costs. This makes it easy to edit when a price increases or decreases. As your business grows and you're able to purchase coconut oil, for example, in a five gallon bucket instead of 1 gallon at a time, your price per ounce will decrease, which will give you a little more profit.

First you will need to determine ingredient costs used in your formula. As an example, we'll use the Castile soap formula discussed earlier in this book.

INGREDIENT	AMOUNT USED IN FORMULA	COST PER OUNCE	COST
Distilled Water	6 oz.	.01	.06
Sodium Hydroxide	2.4 oz.	.13	.31
Olive Oil	16 oz.	.13	2.08
TOTAL	24.4 oz.		$2.45

Take the total cost of the entire batch and divide it by the number of bars of soap made from the batch. This example makes a 1.5-pound batch (24.4 oz. divided by 16 oz. in a pound), which in this example equals 8 bars of soap. So we divide $2.45 by 8 to come up with a cost per bar: $0.31.

Next we will add the following amounts to the cost per bar:

Equipment/Packaging/Shipping Supplies: $0.25

Overhead: $0.10

Labor: $1.25 - this was calculated at $10/hour at 1 hour to make 8 bars of soap (8 bars/$10 = $1.25 labor/bar).

Add these items together and it comes to a total cost of $1.91 to make each bar of soap. Note that it takes about the same time to make a larger batch of soap as it does to make a smaller batch, so once you have finalized your formula, you can increase your batch size to make 16 bars of soap in almost the same amount of time as it took to make 8 bars of soap. You've now decreased your labor costs, meaning you'll make even more profit on each bar of soap you sell. If you need help calculating a larger batch size, simply contact us and we'll be happy to assist.

Other items to consider that will decrease your costs and increase your profits include:

- Buy ingredients in large quantities. Buying a gallon of olive oil will cost less per ounce than if you buy a 16 oz. bottle. It is a larger upfront cost, but the per-ounce price is significantly lower.

- Consider joining a co-op where members join together to buy ingredients and split the cost. Or you can share ingredients with other local soap making friends. Go in together to purchase a 50 lb. bucket of oil and split it.

- Stick with one basic soap formula base (i.e., the same combination of oils) and simply switch out colorants and scents to make each batch unique.

Now you'll want to set yourself up right in terms of consumer pricing. Do you have an idea of what handmade soaps are selling for in your ideal market? Will you start out selling retail directly to customers, but then want to expand into selling wholesale to boutiques? Regardless, you want to be sure there is enough profit margin, no matter how you sell your soap.

On average, you can double your cost per bar of soap to come up with your wholesale price (the price that a retail store would pay for it). You'd at least double that price again to come up with your retail price (what customers would pay for it on a website, at a craft fair or home party).

For example, if it costs $1 to make a bar of soap, your wholesale price could be $2 and your retail price $4. However, you may want to bump those figures up to account for any increase in ingredient prices, if you needed to hire help to make more soap, or simply increase your profits. Some soap makers will create a standard level of 2.5 times their cost for wholesale and then doubling or even multiplying that wholesale price 2.5 times for their retail price. In the above example, with a $1 cost, the wholesale price would be $2.50 and the retail price $6.25.

This is where you again need to know your market. Are your soaps of high enough quality with high-end packaging, and do they provide results consistent with the retail price you want to charge? If the price is too high for the market, sales will be slow or non-existent. If the price is too low, then you won't make enough money, and may run yourself out of business because funds brought in won't cover cost increases or unexpected expenses.

Also, if prices are set too low, you can *cheapen* yourself; prospective customers might assume your products are of low quality and potentially not purchase them because of this. For example, if you're selling your soaps for $2.50/bar at a market and another booth is selling soaps that look nearly identical for $5.00/bar, some customers will buy the more expensive soap just because they assume the price tag reflects the quality of the soap.

Where to Sell Your Handmade Soaps

There are a number of ways you can sell your handcrafted soaps; it depends on your personality and the time and money you want to invest. Three general areas of selling that will be discussed here include in-person sales venues, online sales and other distribution channels. Many soapers will use a combination of these sales methods in their businesses.

In-Person Sales

In-person sales are just that… standing in front of potential customers and selling your wares. Examples of sales venues may include home parties, farmer's markets, arts and craft shows and even your own retail storefront.

The pros to this type of sales include connecting directly with customers and educating them on the benefits of your soaps, as well as they can touch, smell and see it in person. This can go a long way in creating lasting relationships with customers. We know of soapers who have customers return to their farmer's market booths every month to stock up on soaps for themselves and for gifts.

The drawbacks to these types of sales venues include the time it takes to build enough inventories to stock a table or booth; the time spent setting up displays, selling at the event and breaking down the displays again; and the cost for display materials and entry fees to the show. Retail storefronts have additional expenses including rent, utilities, insurance and staffing costs.

Online Sales

Online sales can be made on a variety of websites; your own branded website or through online marketplace directories. There are a number of popular handmade shopping sites; the most recognizable being Etsy, Artfire and Poppyswap. You can do a quick online search for similar sites, review them and their terms for opening a storefront and then create your own shop within an hour or so.

The benefits to using this type of sales avenue include exposure across the internet on a variety of websites, increased branding strength (your logo and main website are repeated across all of the shopping sites) and the fact that the shopping site will do some *work* for you. The popularity and search engine rankings of these sites provide a steady flow of traffic, which means more exposure for you and your products.

This type of sales venue is also good for those who want to provide excellent products and customer service, but are more comfortable behind the scenes and less a fan of presenting direct sales pitches. Online sales allow people to create great soaps and respond to customer inquiries via email, while no face-to-face interaction is needed.

Some drawbacks include the monetary and time costs of developing and promoting your own website as well as costs associated with selling soaps on another shopping site. Most sites charge a fee to list your item, along with a percentage of the final product sales price. This usually isn't too steep of an expense, but the costs can add up if you're listing a lot of products that aren't selling.

Another disadvantage to selling on shopping sites is standing out among all of the other sellers in the marketplace; making sure your products are noticed through quality photographs, clear descriptions and pricing. Unfortunately, a number of sellers on these types of websites will price their products really low, making it very difficult to compete on price. You have to show potential customers (who don't have the luxury of physically holding and smelling your soap) how your soaps compare and why they are worth every penny you're charging.

Other Distribution Channels

Some other ways you can sell your soaps include creating a direct-sales company structure, where you train consultants who recruit people to hold home parties; hiring sales representatives to secure wholesale accounts; and approaching stores yourself (both online and brick and mortar stores) to carry your products. Each of these ways can expand your *reach*, allowing more customers to learn about and try your products.

The downsides to these sales channels include the time, energy and organization needed to structure and follow up with potential consultants, sales representatives or stores. Another potential drawback is that you won't pocket as much profit from these sales because consultants and sales representatives will earn a commission from each sale, and wholesale accounts purchase products at your wholesale prices. The trade-off may be worth it, as wholesale accounts place larger orders and may do on a regular basis. A store ordering $300 worth of soap every quarter equals to $1200 per year, just from that single store. How long would it take you to sell that amount of soap on your website, where customers may order on average two bars of soap at a time?

Even though you might profit more from website sales because those customers are paying retail prices, it may be a good option for you to consider selling your products via wholesale in order to secure those larger sales on a regular basis.

This section has just scratched the surface on some of the ways in which you can sell your soaps. If you're interested in a consultation to determine which sales avenues are right for you, your personality and sales goals, please contact Alyssa. She can help you determine which methods are suitable and coach you through getting these sales avenues established.

Resource Directory

There are a number of resources for you to tap into as you are developing and growing your soap making business. Of course, we're going to recommend our services first and foremost! Mary is an expert in using goat milk in formulations from soaps to lotions and beyond. Alyssa is an expert in providing bath and body business-specific training, coaching and resources. To get a discount on Alyssa's services, mention that you purchased this book.

Finally, two top-notch industry resources are the Indie Beauty Network and the Handcrafted Soap Makers Guild. Both organizations will help you connect with other soapers around the world, and are great opportunities to keep you informed of new trends in the marketplace, get your questions answered and learn about developments or changes in industry regulations.

Handcrafted Soapmakers Guild
PO Box 5103
Portland, OR 97208
(503) 283-7758
(866) 900-SOAP
www.soapguild.org

Indie Beauty Network
Call to request the mailing address
(704) 291-7280
www.indiebeauty.com

Purchasing Ingredients, Supplies and Packaging

Below are reputable companies we recommend when buying ingredients and supplies. While many supply companies are out there, only stores we have shopped with, and had a positive experience with, are listed.

Brambleberry Soap Making Supplies

2138 Humboldt Street

Bellingham, WA 98225

(360) 734-8278

(877) 627-7883

www.brambleberry.com

Camden Grey Essential Oils Inc.

3579 NW 82nd Avenue

Doral, FL 33122

(305) 500-9630

www.camdengrey.com

Essential Wholesale

2211 NW Nicolai St

Portland, OR 97210

(503) 722-7557

(866) 252-9639

www.essentialwholesale.com

From Nature With Love

Natural Sourcing, LLC

341 Christian Street

Oxford, CT 06478

(203) 702-2500

(800) 520-2060

www.fromnaturewithlove.com

Glenbrook Farms

1538 Shiloh Road

Campbellsville, KY 42718

(888) 716-7627

www.glenbrookfarm.com

Mountain Rose Herbs

PO Box 50220

Eugene, OR 97405

(541) 741-7307

(800) 879-3337

www.mountainroseherbs.com

Nature's Garden

42109 State Route 18

Wellington, OH 44090

440-647-0100

866-647-2368

www.naturesgardencandles.com

New Directions Aromatics

60 Industrial Parkway, Suite 325

Cheektowaga, NY 14227

(800) 246-7817

www.newdirectionsaromatics.com

Soapers Choice

30 E. Oakton Street

Des Plaines, IL 60018

(800) 322-6457, ext. 8930

www.soaperschoice.com

Soap Making Resource

355 E Liberty St. Suite C

Lancaster, PA 17602

717-875-8670

www.soap-making-resource.com

The Original Soap Dish

PO Box 263

South Whitley, IN 46787

(260) 723-4039

www.soap-dish.com

Wholesale Supplies Plus

10035 Broadview Road

Broadview Heights, OH 44147

(800) 359-0944

www.wholesalesuppliesplus.com

Glossary

A

Abrasives: Also called an exfoliant. Gritty or rough ingredients that are added to soap to help scrub away dirt or dead outer skin cells.

Absolute: A concentrated, highly aromatic mixture extracted from plants via alcohol and vacuum distillation. Absolutes are an alcohol soluble aromatic base.

Acid: A substance with a pH less than 7.

Additives: Any ingredient other than water, lye, oils or butters that is added to soap. Examples include colorants, herbs, fragrance or essential oils, and antioxidants.

Alkali: Also called a base. A substance with a pH greater than 7. An alkali can be used to neutralize an acid. Sodium hydroxide (lye) is an alkali.

Allergen: A substance that can cause an allergic reaction. Using nut oils (peanut, hazelnut, shea butter) in soap can cause a person with nut allergies to have an allergic reaction.

Antibacterial: A substance that can effectively destroy bacteria.

Antioxidant: Prevents or slows oxidation. In soaping, these substances help block the process of oxygen reacting with oils and causing them to go rancid. Antioxidant properties in soap help prolong the life of the oils in your soap. Examples of antioxidants include Vitamin E and Rosemary Oleoresin Extract. Some oils have naturally high levels of Vitamin E, including high oleic sunflower or wheat germ oil, and are added to formulas to help prolong the lives of other oils in the formula. Antioxidants are <u>not</u> the same as preservatives.

Antiseptic: A substance that has the ability to fight infection.

Aromatherapy: The use of fragrance or essences from plants to alter a person's mental or emotional well-being.

Aromatic: Having a strong fragrance or odor.

Astringent: A substance used to tighten skin and remove excess oil from skin.

Attar: Also known as otto. An expensive, highly concentrated essential oil obtained from flower petals.

B

Base: The alkali used in soap making, such as sodium hydroxide (lye).

Base Oils: Also known as fixed oils; these are the main oils that make up the soap formula, such as coconut, palm and olive oils.

Botanical: A substance obtained from a plant's parts.

Botanical Name: Also known as the International Nomenclature of Cosmetics Ingredients (INCI) name. The Latin name assigned to distinguish one species from another, the scientific name composed of the genus followed by the species.

C

Carrier Oil: A vegetable or nut base oil used to dilute essential oils prior to applying to the skin.

Castile: A region in Spain known for producing olive oil based soaps in the 13th century. Today, a soap made with 100% olive oil is referred to as a Castile soap. Some soapers call a soap with *mostly* olive oil Castile.

Caustic: A corrosive substance that burns through a chemical action. Caustic can refer to an acid or a base but is typically used to describe the action of an alkaline base. Sodium hydroxide (lye) is caustic.

Caustic Potash: Also known as potassium hydroxide. This is the alkali (base) used in liquid soap making.

Caustic Soda: Also known as sodium hydroxide (lye). This is the alkali (base) used in bar soap making.

Cold Kettle: Also known as cold process. Refers to a type of soap making in which oils and lye are mixed at about the same temperature to start the saponification process.

Cold Pressed: A method for extracting oils from raw materials. Oil is extracted through mechanical pressure at low temperatures, typically less than 125° Fahrenheit. Cold pressing preserves the benefits and properties of the oils.

Cold Process: Also known as cold kettle or CP. A method of soap making without utilizing any external heat source other than to melt the hard oils.

Comedogenic: A substance that may clog pores and produce and/or aggravate acne.

Concrete: A thick, fragrant material extracted from a plant base through solvent extraction; contains the essential oils, fatty acids and wax from the plant base.

Cosmetic: A product applied to the human body for cleansing, beautifying, promoting attractiveness, or altering the appearance. Products deemed cosmetics are regulated in the United States by the Food and Drug Administration.

Cosmetic Grade: A designation by the U.S. government that the product has been approved for use directly on the skin.

Crock Pot Hot Process: Also called CPHP, a method of soap making using the heat from an electric crock pot during the soap making process.

Cruelty Free: Not tested on animals.

Cure: Also known as the aging process of soap. This is the time period between making the soap and using the soap. Soap should cure for at least 4-6 weeks before it is used. During this time, the soap becomes mild and excess water evaporates, making the bar harden and last longer.

D

D&C: An acronym that stands for Drugs & Cosmetics. The term is used to designate the U.S. government's approved use in drugs (external use only) and cosmetics, such as D&C Red #7.

Decoction: An extract of brewed hard plant material such as bark or root. Extracted by boiling the plant material to obtain various properties.

Deodorize: To remove scent. Some oils are refined and deodorized before selling to remove the scent so that they do not bring an additional odor to the finished product in which the oil is used.

Detergent: A surfactant that acts similarly to soap in terms of cleansing, but is not created by the saponification of fats and oils.

Dreaded Orange Spots: Small yellow-orange spots that appear on the surface of cold processed soap; primarily thought to be a result of unsaponified oils going rancid. Also called DOS. DOS is more prevalent in highly superfatted soaps.

Discounted Water Cold Process: A cold process method of soap making using a lower percentage of water in the formula for a stronger lye solution. Also called DWCP.

E

Emollient: A substance used to soften or soothe skin. Examples include shea or cocoa butter, and glycerin.

Enfleurage: The process of extracting the aromatic essences from plants using odorless fats to absorb oils from flowers. The fat is then dissolved in alcohol to separate the essence from the fat and distilled to remove the alcohol.

Essential Oil: A highly concentrated, volatile oil extracted from aromatic plants, most commonly through pressing or steam distillation. Also called EO.

Exfoliant: Also known as an abrasive. Gritty or rough ingredients added to soap to help scrub away dirt or dead outer skin cells.

Exothermic: A chemical reaction that releases heat. Soap is made as the product of an exothermic reaction between lye and fat (oils).

Expeller Pressed: The mechanical method for extracting oils from raw materials. Oil is extracted from a base by mechanically crushing and pressing the material at temperatures of less than 210° Fahrenheit.

Extract: A substance, extracted from a plant through distillation, pressure or solvents, containing its essence in concentrated form.

F

Fatty Acids: Compounds of carbon, oxygen and hydrogen found in fats and oils. They can be saturated or unsaturated, and in soap, fatty acids are what give soap their bubbly lathers, hardness, cleansing and conditioning characteristics.

FD&C: An acronym that stands for Food, Drugs & Cosmetics. The term is used to designate the U.S. government's approved use in food, drugs (external use only) and cosmetics.

Fixed Oils: Also known as base oils, these are the main oils that make up the soap formula, such as coconut, palm and olive oils.

Flash Point: The lowest temperature at which the vapors of a liquid can ignite. Some fixed oils and essential oils have low flash points, so soap makers must be aware of this during the soap making process, as items with low flash points can burst into flames when heated.

French Milled Soap: Also known as hand milled. Pre-made soap is grated, mixed with liquids, gently heated and pressed into molds.

Formula: A listing of ingredients in fixed proportions, typically expressed in percentages.

Fragrance Oil: Synthetically scented oil formulated to mimic natural fragrances. Used when a particular scent cannot be created naturally, i.e. by essential oils. Also called FO.

G

Gel: Also known as gel phase or gel stage. An early phase of the saponification process when the temperature of the soap batter increases after being poured into the mold. The soap temporarily becomes a translucent gel and slowly returns to a solid, cooler mass. Not all soap batches go through a gel phase. Some soap makers prefer their soaps to gel and others do not. It is a matter of personal preference.

Glycerin: A thick, sticky, clear substance naturally created during the process of saponification. Glycerin has emollient and humectant properties. Handmade cold process and hot process soaps retain the glycerin created in the soap making process. Commercial soaps often remove the glycerin from their final product.

H

Handmade Soap: Soap made by combining base oil(s) with an alkali using traditional methods including hot and cold processing.

Hand Milled: Also known as French Milled. Pre-made soap is grated, mixed with liquids, gently heated and pressed into molds.

Herb: An aromatic plant that does not produce woody tissue, and usually dies back at the end of the growing season.

Hot Process: Also known as HP. A method of soap making that uses heat to speed up the saponification process.

Humectant: A substance that attracts and retains moisture, such as glycerin.

Hydrogenated Oil: Unsaturated oils with added hydrogen to create a solid oil that is more resistant to spoiling.

Hydrogenation: A chemical process of converting a vegetable oil from a liquid into a solid using hydrogen.

Hydrosol: Also known as floral water. When a distiller steam brews plant material the oil is collected as an essential oil. The remaining water is collected as a hydrosol. Hydrosols are not highly concentrated, so they are not suitable for cold processed soap formulations.

Hygroscopic: The tendency of a material to absorb and retain moisture from the air. Sodium hydroxide (lye) has hygroscopic properties.

Hypoallergenic: A substance unlikely to cause an allergic reaction.

I

Industrial Nomenclature of Cosmetic Ingredients: A system of names for ingredients that must be used when labeling soaps and cosmetics. Each country has different regulations regarding when the INCI name must be included on product labels. Also known as INCI.

Industrial Grade: A designation by the U.S. government that refers to the intended use of a product. Industrial grade products are not intended for use directly on the skin. **Do not use industrial grade ingredients in soap or cosmetic making**; use Cosmetic Grade ingredients instead.

Infusion: A liquid extract made by steeping botanical matter in oil or water to extract various properties of the plant material.

Insoluble: A substance that is incapable of being dissolved in a liquid such as water or alcohol.

Irritant: A substance that can cause irritation or inflammation of the skin.

L

Litmus paper: A strip of paper containing a mixture of water-soluble dyes used to indicate the pH level of a substance. Blue litmus paper turns red under acidic conditions and red litmus paper turns blue under alkaline conditions. Neutral litmus paper is purple. Litmus paper simply determines whether a solution is acidic or alkaline, it does not measure the strength of the acid or base.

Lye: Also known as sodium hydroxide or caustic soda. This is the alkali (base) used in bar soap making.

M

Manufacturer's Grade: A designation by the U.S. government that the product has been approved for use in the manufacturing of another product. These products have not been approved for direct application on the skin, but they can be used when making soap or candles. Some fragrance oils come in manufacturer's grades.

Melt and Pour Soap: A pre-made soap base designed to melt, mix with certain additives and pour into molds. The soap is ready to be used once it hardens.

Melting Point: The temperature at which a solid becomes a liquid.

Material Safety Data Sheet or Safety Data Sheet: A report provided by the manufacturer or distributor to define the health, safety and fire risks associated with a substance and outlines how to handle and work with the substance in a safe manner. Also known as MSDS or SDS.

N

NaOH: The molecular formula for Sodium Hydroxide, also known as Lye or Caustic Soda.

Nonvolatile: A substance that does not easily evaporate.

O

Organic: A substance that at one time was alive and has not had chemicals or synthetic materials introduced to it.

Oxidation: A chemical reaction with oxygen. In soap making, oxidation of oils can cause the oil to go rancid. Using antioxidants in the soap formula may inhibit oxidation and help prevent Dreaded Orange Spots in the soap.

P

pH: A measurement of the acidity or alkalinity of a substance. The scale ranges from 0 (highly acidic) to 14 (highly alkaline or highly basic). A pH value of 7 is neutral, a pH less than 7 is acidic and a pH of more than 7 is alkaline, also called basic. Sodium Hydroxide, or lye has a pH of 14. Water has a pH of 7. Most cured soaps have a pH range of 8-10.

pH Test Strip: A strip of special paper used to determine the approximate pH of a substance.

Photosensitizer: A substance that can cause skin to be more prone to sunburn when exposed to sunlight.

Potassium Hydroxide: Also known as Caustic Potash, this is the alkali (base) used in liquid soap making.

Preservative: A substance capable of inhibiting bacterial or mold growth.

R

Rancidity: Having an unpleasant, stale smell, as a result of decomposition or spoilage.

Refined: The process of removing impurities from the natural base.

Rendering: The process of heating lard or tallow to a liquid state to remove solids or impurities.

Room Temperature Cold Process: A cold process soap making method that calls for oils to be at room temperature when the lye solution is added. Also known as RTCP.

S

Saponification Value: The amount of milligrams of sodium hydroxide required to saponify 1 gram of fat (oil). Can also be abbreviated to SAP Value.

Saponification: The chemical reaction between a base (fat or oil) and an alkali (sodium hydroxide/lye) to produce a salt (soap) and a free alcohol (glycerin).

Sebum: The fatty substance secreted by the sebaceous glands of the skin. Sebum is the skin's natural oil.

Seizing: The unexpected solidifying of soap batter during processing, making it unable to be mixed or poured. Seizing results from using some fragrance or essential oils, waxes or the temperature of the oils in the soap batter.

Soap: A simple cleansing agent; the sodium salt resulting from the combination of oils and fats with an alkali.

Soda Ash: A harmless, but unsightly powdery white residue that can form on the surface of soap. It may result from excess oxygen exposure during the cooling and curing process. Soap with soda ash may be used as is, but the ash can be cut off the soap for a more visually appealing bar.

Sodium Hydroxide: Also known as NaOH, lye or caustic soda, this is the alkali (base) used in bar soap making.

Soluble: A substance that is capable of being dissolved or liquefied.

Solvent Extraction: A method for extracting oils from raw materials. Oil is separated from the base using a liquid solvent. The oil is then distilled and the solvent evaporates, leaving only the oil.

Steam Distillation: The steam and pressure method used to extract essential oils from plant materials.

Superfatting: The addition of additional oils or butters; remaining unsaponified within the finished soap. These excess oils and butters contribute to the moisturizing properties of the soap.

Surfactant: A substance that reduces the surface tension of the liquid in which it is dissolved. A surfactant assists in releasing dirt and oils from surfaces when water is added.

Synthetic: A substance that is artificially produced, not of natural origin.

T

Tocopherol: Any of the four forms (alpha-, beta-, delta- or gamma-) of Vitamin E, an antioxidant added to soaps as an emollient and antioxidant. Alpha-tocopherol has greatest amount of vitamin E.

Trace: A point in soap making where the mixture reaches a noticeable thickness. Trace is often recognized when the soap is drizzled upon itself and leaves a trail before disappearing back into the mixture.

U

Unrefined: The natural, unaltered base, such as the oil obtained from the first pressing.

Unsaponifiables: Components that do not react with sodium hydroxide during saponification and remain in its original state. These components contribute moisturizing or other skin nourishing properties to the finished soap.

V

Vegan: not containing any animal parts such as lard or tallow, or any ingredients produced by animals, such as beeswax or silk.

Vegetarian: Not containing any animal parts, such as lard or tallow.

Vegetable Shortening: A solid fat made by hydrogenating vegetable oils.

Viscosity: A measurement of the resistance of a substance to flow. It is commonly referred to as thickness or resistance to pouring.

Volatile Oils: Oils that evaporate or vaporize easily. Essential oils are highly volatile.

W

Water Soluble: A substance that is dissolvable in water.

Wildcrafted: Refers to herbs and botanicals grown in the wild without the use of pesticides or other chemicals.